China:
From the First Chinese
to the Olympics

Alden R. Carter

ISBN 978-1-60145-399-0

Photograph Credits. 39degN: 24*; A-giâu: 164; Saad Akhtar: 74; Captmic; 60*; Carol Shadis Carter: 5, 9, 12, 14, 15, 16, 17, 18, 27, 36, 48, 122, 123, 125, 174, 182; Richard Chambers: 7; Allen Timothy Chang: 21; Chang Liu: 127*; Colegota: 190; Creative Commons (no acknowledgment): 98; Robert Croma: 130, 138, 139, 141; David: 149; de:Benutzer:Pakxé: 114; DF08: 128, 175; diegodepol: 19; Steve Evans: 105*; F3rn4nd0: 156; Luca Galuzzi (www.galuzzi.it): 144; Hector Garcia: 172; André Holdrinet: 26*; Insignifica: 6; JakeLMJake: 180; Jialiang Gao: 107*; Jiang: 133; G.S.K.Lee: 162; Rüdiger Meier: 154; Montrasio Medi: 192; Peter Morgan: 92*; Mountain: 29 (Shanghai Museum), 43 (Shanghai Museum); Rolf Müller: 91*; Nowozin: 135; Tietew: 166; Tokugawapants: 111; Tuxnduke: 58*; Gert Wrigge and Anton Oettl: 151*; Yaohua2000: 177; Yaoleilei: 10; Zhang2008: 185; Zhuwq: 45. All other photographs either public domain or fair comment. *Licensed through Creative Commons GDFL license.

Parts of this book were previously published in *China Past–China Future* (Franklin Watts, 1994) and in *Modern China* (Franklin Watts, 1986) both by Alden R. Carter.

Cover photograph by Tee Meng (Creative Commons, GDFL license). Cover design by Brian P. Carter.

Map courtesy of University of Texas Libraries.

Printed in the United States of America.

Booklocker.com, Inc.
2008

About Alden R. Carter

Alden R. Carter is the author of eleven novels and thirty nonfiction books. The author of two previous books on China, his *China Past-China Future* (1994) received honors from New York Public Library, the Council for Wisconsin Writers, and the Information Division of the Taipei Economic & Cultural Office, Republic of China. He recently co-authored Dr. Chang's memoir of growing up in China. He resides in Marshfield, Wisconsin, with his wife, the photographer Carol Shadis Carter. They have two grown children, Brian and Siri.

About David W. Chang

Dr. David Wen-Wei Chang is one of America's distinguished China scholars. In a forty-year career, he has taught in the United States, Taiwan, and the People's Republic. He is the author of five scholarly books and numerous articles in the field of China studies. His memoir of growing up in China, *At My Mother's Grave: A Memoir of War-torn China*, will be published in 2008.

Acknowledgments

Many thanks to all who helped with *China: From the First Chinese to the Olympics*, particularly David and Alice Chang, my wife, Carol, our children Brian and Siri, and our China traveling companions Don and Georgette Beyer. Thanks also to the editors of Wikipedia and all the photographers who have made their work available through Creative Commons, the photography index of Wikipedia.com. Thanks also to Robert Croma for forwarding high-resolution copies of his extraordinary pictures of the Tiananmen Square demonstrations.

**For the Changs
and all who work for a better understanding
between East and West**

Table of Contents

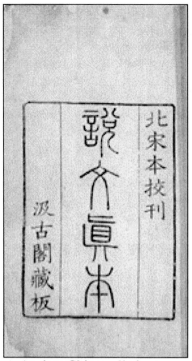

Ancient Chinese dictionary

The Spelling and Pronunciation of Chinese Words

Unlike English words, Chinese words are not spelled with letters representing spoken sounds. Instead, each word is written as an ideogram (or character) representing an idea. By combining various characters, different ideas can be expressed. For example: the character for *speak* and the character for *bright* together mean *explanation*.

Chinese has at least 50,000 ideograms, and probably no one knows them all. About 6,000 characters are commonly used, and the government has simplified about 3,000 to ease the task of learning written Chinese. Literacy is particularly valuable in China because the pronunciation of Chinese varies widely from region to region while the written language is universal. All schools in China now teach Mandarin, the most widely spoken dialect, as part of an effort to standardize pronunciation.

A number of systems have been devised to spell Chinese words in the Latin alphabet used in most of the West. Chinese words in this book are spelled according to the pinyin system adopted by the State Council of the People's Republic of China in 1979 to replace the Wade-Giles system developed in Great Britain in the 19th century. Since Chinese is a tonal language, no system can exactly duplicate the actual spoken sounds of Chinese words. Nevertheless, a fair approximation can be made by using the equivalent English sounds for pinyin consonants, with these exceptions:

c is pronounced *ts* when it is the initial sound in a word

q is pronounced *ch*

x is pronounced as a soft *sh*, nearly *sy*

z is pronounced *dz*

zh is pronounced *j*

Chinese vowels are most commonly pronounced:

a as in the *ah* in *far*

e as in the *eh* in *bet*

i as in the *ee* in *free*, except when it is a final vowel following *c*, *s*, or *z* when it is pronounced *uh*, or after *ch*, *sh*, or *zh* when it becomes *ur*

o as in the *aw* in *law*

u as in the *oo* in *pool*

When two vowels are written together, each retains an individual sound. Hence, *Mao* is pronounced like the *mou* in *mouth*.

Forward
by David Wen-Wei Chang, Ph.D.

Since Marco Polo dictated his famous travelogue seven hundred years ago, Western readers have come to know China through thousands of books and countless articles. Yet China remains an enigma to most Westerners. It is vital to the future of an interconnected world for writers, scholars, and all people of good will to continue their efforts to correct the misconceptions, untruths, and prejudices that have so long plagued the relationship between China and the West. It is my hope that Alden R. Carter's *China: From the First Chinese to the Olympics* will introduce great numbers of Americans to China's history, present reality, and hopes for the future—a future in which America and the rest of the world will have an increasingly significant interest.

It is difficult for Americans, accustomed as they are to a rapidly changing society where the past often seems irrelevant, to appreciate the incredible length of China's unique history and the durability of so many of its political and cultural institutions. Until the early 20th century, China's governmental, social, and economic framework had changed little in over 2,000 years, despite devastating invasions, frequent internal rebellions, and a multitude of natural disasters. With the exception of India, no other major nation has known such an enduring continuity from the ancient past to the threshold of the modern era.

In the 20th century, China was convulsed by three great revolutions. Dr. Sun Yat-sen's Nationalist Revolution of 1911 held out the promise of Western-style democracy in China. But Japanese aggression, Western indifference, and China's own unreadiness combined to doom Dr. Sun's vision. The Communist revolution of 1949 succeeded in unifying the nation and ridding China of foreign interference in its internal affairs. But Mao Zedong's radical social and economic agenda became a monumental disaster. Only the counterbalance of Premier Zhou Enlai and his fellow pragmatists prevented the Chinese state from capsizing during the stormy era that ended with the death of Mao in 1976.

The third great revolution began in 1978 when the reformers led by Deng Xiaoping took direction of China's development. What has happened since has been, in its way, every bit as startling as the first two revolutions. Rejecting the commune system and the Maoist philosophy of perpetual revolution, the reformers adopted a "socialist market economy" that has transformed China in a mere thirty years into one of the world's leading economic powers. Yet this revolution has not been without blood and huge social costs. The Tiananmen Square massacre in 1989 and the repression of the Democracy Movement set back the dreams of democratic reform for this generation and perhaps the next one as well. Economic development has disrupted age-old Chinese attitudes of cooperative effort in urban neighborhoods and rural villages alike. Environmental degradation threatens all China has accomplished in economic terms since 1978.

As I approach eighty, I can view China from a long perspective if not the peace I might have hoped for had my homeland moved decisively in the direction of participatory and pluralistic democracy in the last decades of the 20th century. For a century now, the Chinese have known almost constant revolution. I was born in 1929 or 1930 (family records are unclear) in the midst of a great famine on the eve of the Japanese invasion of China. My boyhood and young manhood were spent in a China convulsed by foreign aggression and civil war. My second oldest brother was killed in Manchuria in 1948 during the fighting between the Nationalists and the Communists. I was in Shanghai, where my mother was receiving medical treatment, when the Communists took control of the city in May 1949. Soon after, security agents forced me to carry an offer of negotiations to my eldest brother, a Nationalist general in command of one of the offshore islands. He not only refused to listen but refused to allow me to return to the Mainland to care for our mother. That evening I became an unwilling refugee from my homeland.

Four years later, I came to the United States as a student with the full intention of soon returning to China. While I studied and taught in the United States and my eldest brother served in the Nationalist army on Taiwan, my third brother worked as a farmer in the People's Republic of China (PRC). For him, life was most difficult as he suffered years of humiliation at the hands of the Communist authorities for his relationship to us and because he had owned a few more acres than the average farmer before the revolution.

Communication with families in the PRC was so difficult in the quarter century following the Communist revolution that I did not learn of my mother's death in 1955 until nearly twenty years later. Through the 1960's and 1970's, I wrote and taught about China, hoping that my experience in two cultures would help bridge the gulf between them. In 1968, I became a United States citizen. Finally, in 1979, with relations improving between the United States and the PRC, I was at last able to return to China to visit my mother's grave and to see again some of the relatives I had left behind.

I offer my story only as a mild example of what millions of Chinese suffered in a century of upheaval the like of which few in the United States can imagine. Since China again opened its doors, I have returned a dozen times to study firsthand the immense changes in China, and to share with the citizens of my homeland something of what I have learned in six decades of living in the West. It has been my privilege to lecture to large numbers of students and intellectuals, and to meet on frequent occasions with scholars and government leaders for whom the United States often seems as impenetrable an enigma as China seems to American intellectuals and officials.

It has also been my privilege to guide university groups of professors, public school teachers, and other interested Americans on their first visits to China. On one of these trips, I was joined by the writer Alden Carter and his photographer–social worker wife, Carol, who were gathering material for a book on China. Carol's job was difficult because many Chinese dislike having their pictures taken by strangers, and the incredible diversity of China is exceedingly difficult to capture on film. Yet Carol, with her disarming smile and her sharp eye for the best image and angle, managed to capture both the people and the physical reality of China.

While Carol snapped roll after roll of film, Al asked a flood of questions. His insatiable curiosity, his demand for exhaustive and rigorously accurate answers, and his intuitive ability to enter into the spirit of what it means to be Chinese made *Modern China* (Franklin Watts, 1986) a joy to read and, with Carol's photographs, an invaluable resource for young people.

Some years later, it was again my pleasure to read and comment on the manuscript for *China Past–China Future* (Franklin Watts, 1994), Carter's concise introduction for readers of all ages to the history and political, cultural, and social institutions of China.

Carter's third book on China, *China: From the First Chinese to the Olympics*, examines the history of China as background for a detailed picture of the stunning developments wrought by economic reform in China in the past three decades. Carter ends his account with a clear and insightful look at the probable shape of China's future.

China has known terrible suffering in the last century. Yet, even in the worst of times, the resiliency, courage, and adaptability of the Chinese people remained unshaken. I share Alden Carter's optimism that the liberalization of the Chinese economy must eventually lead to a more open and democratic China. It is my hope—as it is Carter's—that the coming decades will celebrate the dawn of a new era in the history of East and West; that the generation now growing to adulthood will reach out across the barriers that separated all previous generations to build a world of peace, fairness, and mutual understanding. As a small but significant step in that process, I invite readers to turn now to *China: From the First Chinese to the Olympics*, Alden Carter's stirring account of China's history of glory and suffering, of its challenging present and extraordinary potential for the future, and of the eternal courage and dignity of the Chinese people.

David Wen-Wei Chang
Frederick, Maryland
December 2007

Introduction

From the air, Beijing's Olympic stadium seems to float on the land, an immense bird's nest of intertwining buttresses and girders that seems made as much of wind and sunlight as concrete and steel. Unlike the glowering barrier of the Great Wall, a few dozen miles to the north, this structure welcomes the visitor to China. Here, the stadium seems to announce, is a changed China, a China fully involved with the community of nations as partner, competitor, and powerful voice in the making of the 21st century.

A nation that repelled contact with the outside world for millennia is projecting a new image with China's first Olympic games. This is far more than an exercise in public relations. In the last three decades, China has changed in ways unimaginable at the death of Mao Zedong (1893–1976). Within two years of the death of China's great revolutionary leader, reformers had set a new course for China's development. What was then an impoverished nation locked in a cycle of political upheaval is today one of the world's economic powerhouses wielding immense influence beyond China's borders.

Since 1978 and the beginning of the "reformist" era under Deng Xiaoping (1904–1997), the gross national product (GNP) of China has risen at an astonishing rate of 9% per year. Annual exports have increased from less than $10 billion to some $600 billion. In 1978, China could count only $1.6 billion in foreign currency reserves, today the figure is $1.3 trillion. For most Chinese, incomes have kept pace. Households that once saved for a radio today own a color television, a computer, cell phones, and an air conditioner—virtually unknown luxuries a decade ago. Increasingly, urban and even rural families are considering buying a car.

For all the economic progress, China still has a baffling list of problems. Critical natural resources—even water—are running short. China has plentiful coal to power industry, but the resulting air and water pollution threatens the health of hundreds of millions. Workweeks are long and safety standards for both workers and consumers lacking in many industries. Older plants have become a drain on the economy, their closing threatening the livelihood of huge numbers of workers. A health system that was once available to every person in China has fallen into disrepair. Crime is on the rise. Urban housing developments have forced thousands from their affordable homes. Income disparities between rich and poor households, urban and rural communities, and coastal and inland provinces threaten the social harmony so treasured in Chinese culture. Tens of millions of people still live in poverty. The continued

1

growth in population may in the not too distant future overwhelm China's ability to feed itself.

Although China has reached out diplomatically in recent years, much of the world remains suspicious. Powerful political voices in the United States denounce China as both an economic and military threat. North Korea has become a nuclear power on China's doorstep, asserting its independence from traditional Chinese influence. Attempts to reunify Mainland China and Taiwan have failed with the democratic government of Taiwan increasingly inclined toward permanent separation. Separatists in Tibet and China's far western province of Xinjiang have reportedly sought the aid of international terrorist organizations.

Despite China's miraculous economic success in recent years, a large segment of the Chinese people oppose the continued rule of the Chinese Communist Party. The bloody crackdown on the Democracy Movement following the Tiananmen Square demonstrations of 1989 remains a deep source of resentment. Today the Party allows limited democracy on the local level, but wider participation in Party and governmental affairs remains closed to all but Party members. If and for how long the Party can retain its control will determine the shape of China's affairs in the coming decades.

Two centuries ago, Napoleon cautioned, "Let China sleep for when she awakes, she will shake the world." Today the Chinese dragon is awake. Whether the dragon will be the fire-breathing destroyer portrayed in Western myth or the benevolent bringer of good fortune found in Eastern folklore remains a question for the world at large and the Chinese people themselves.

Chapter 1
China: Most Populous Nation on Earth

More than 1.3 billion people—roughly one out of every five people on earth—live in the People's Republic of China, making it by the far the most populous nation on earth. About 60% of the people reside in rural areas, the vast majority working as farmers. (In the United States fewer than three people in a hundred are farmers.)

Over 92% of the Chinese are members of the Han race, named after an ancient royal family so respected by its subjects that they began calling themselves the "children of Han." Most Han Chinese are shorter and slighter than the average person in Western nations such as the United States, but there are also many tall and big-boned people. Although almost all Han Chinese have brown eyes and straight black hair, skin coloring and facial features vary widely.

In addition to the Han majority, some 55 minorities live in the PRC. Some minorities number only a few thousand while others have millions of members. Most of the minorities make their homes in the vast, sparsely populated western and northwestern regions of China. The hardy Tibetans live "on the roof of the world"—a high plateau north of the Himalayas. Much farther north China's Mongols live in a land of wide prairies called steppes. The Dai people live in tropical Yunnan, bordering Vietnam. Many of the Hakka minority live on colorful fishing boats on the southern coast and rarely go ashore. Some of the minorities were originally independent peoples whose homelands were absorbed by the Chinese empire. Others were immigrants from distant lands who came originally to conquer or to trade. Still others are racially Han Chinese but long ago adopted religions and accompanying lifestyles far different from the Han majority.

POPULATION CONTROL

In 1979, with population growth threatening to outstrip China's resources, the government introduced a vigorous campaign of population control. Today, billboards, posters, newspapers, and radio announcements preach the government's one-child-per-family policy, late marriage, and the use of birth control. The birth of a second child may cause the family to lose access to educational and social benefits. If a woman becomes pregnant a third time, the government pressures the couple to abort the pregnancy and to undergo sterilization. By 2050, the government hopes to stabilize the population at 1.6 billion. The government's population planners battle deeply rooted traditions. For centuries, rural Chinese considered large families a blessing. With few laborsaving machines, many hands were needed to raise a crop. Famine, disease, and war cost the lives of many children long before they reached adulthood, so a large family was necessary to guarantee security for the parents in old age.

"Don't Abandon Baby Girls!" An example of the government's campaign against the "boy preference."

Since the responsibility of caring for aged parents fell to the eldest surviving son, male children were much preferred. As in many other cultures, unwanted female infants or sickly male infants were sometimes drowned or left exposed to the elements to die. Parents arranged marriages, and a young couple often entered into marriage as total strangers. Once the bride entered her in-laws' home, she would remain subservient to her mother-in-law for years, in many cases not leaving the family compound for the rest of her life.

Although arranged marriages and many of the other confining traditions are now outlawed, the preference for boys remains strong. The government has put great effort into convincing Chinese parents of the equal worth of girls, but the persistence of "the boy preference" has made it necessary to add flexibility to the one-child-per-family policy. Parents in rural areas can now have a second child without penalty if their first is a girl or born physically handicapped. National minorities are largely exempt from population control.

With the decline in the birth rate, some population experts worry that China will have a serious shortage of working-age people to support a large elderly population in the second quarter of the 21st century. However, more optimistic experts predict that the introduction of modern technology and more efficient production methods will enable China to bridge the time when the age of the population is out of balance.

Grandmother and grandchild

GEOGRAPHY

In area, the People's Republic of China is one of the world's largest nations, slightly larger than the United States. (Only Russia and Canada are bigger.) Including the island of Taiwan, which has had a separate government since 1949, China has an area of 3,696,100 sq. miles (9,572,900 sq. km). Almost every kind of geography can be found in China: steppes, deserts, mountains, tropical lowlands, pine forests, and flood-washed river valleys. In all, about two-thirds of China is either mountainous or desert.

Many types of climate reflect China's geographical diversity. The south is very wet and hot much of the year. North of the Yangzi River, summers are milder and winters are dry and cold. In Tibet and Mongolia, temperatures plunge far below zero in winter. In the western deserts, there are areas where it will not rain for years and summer temperatures climb over 100 F (38 C).

The PRC is divided into twenty-two provinces, four self-governing municipalities (the capital Beijing and the huge cities of Tianjin, Chongqing, and Shanghai), five autonomous regions, and two special administrative regions (the former British colony of Hong Kong and the former Portuguese colony of Macao).

Police before Potala Palace in Lhasa, Tibet

Eastern China has some of the most heavily populated areas on earth. About 90% of the population lives on only 30% of the land. Half of China is sparsely settled. China's minorities live mainly in the autonomous regions of Inner Mongolia, Ningxia, Guangxi, Xinjiang, and Tibet. The regions enjoy no true self-government, and the term autonomous refers only to cultural autonomy. Despite a stated policy of preserving minority cultures, the government of the People's Republic has promoted extensive migration of Han Chinese to the autonomous regions. Today, native peoples are the majority only in Tibet and Xinjiang. For many centuries, Tibet was an independent nation, and Tibetans and world opinion still favor a return to independence. Neighboring Xinjiang likewise has an independence movement. Neither seems likely to succeed against the overwhelming power of the PRC.

RIVERS OF SORROW AND LIFE

China's great rivers have played a major part in Chinese history. The most famous is the Yangzi (Chang Jiang), which divides southern from central China. Some 3,950 miles (6,360 km) long, the Yangzi is the third longest river in the world after the Nile and the Amazon. The Yangzi is a great thoroughfare for ships and boats carrying goods and passengers through an area that is home for some 400 million people. Near the coast the river is 30 miles (48 km) wide and deep enough for oceangoing tankers and freighters steaming upriver to China's largest city, the port of Shanghai.

Boatyard on the Yangtze

Another mighty river divides central from northern China. The Yellow River, or Huang Ho, was known for generations as "the river of sorrows." It has flooded 1,500 times in recorded history, killing hundreds of thousands and driving millions from their homes. Yet the river is a blessing to the people, too. Every year its waters carry millions of tons of silt down from the northwestern highlands. The silt turns the water a deep yellow, giving the river its name. The river deposits the silt as a rich layer of soil on the flood plain, producing incredibly fertile farmland.

Many of China's rivers have become seriously polluted by industrial waste, sewage, and agricultural runoff. The building of great dams on the Yangzi has endangered the survival of several species of fish and threatened the livelihood of tens of thousands of fishing families. Irrigation and the demands of cities and factories have so depleted the Yellow River that twice in recent years its waters have not reached the ocean.

China's many rivers empty into the Pacific Ocean. China has a 4,000-mile (6,440-km) coastline, and the Chinese have long used the coastal waters for fishing and trading. In the era of modernization, the government has placed a huge emphasis on China's ports and merchant fleet. Today, China has the most modern containerized cargo handling facilities in the world. Its merchant fleet is among the world's largest, handling the great majority of China's trade with other nations.

NATURAL RESOURCES

China has a shortage of good farmland. Only about 10% of the country is well suited to farming and this amount is falling as highway construction and urban growth devour precious acreage. Land that would be rejected as completely unsuitable for agriculture in many countries is farmed with great care and skill by China's farmers, generally known as peasants. In many areas, they have sculpted low mountains into terraces to gain more farmland.

China has vast natural resources for energy and industry. China is the world's second largest consumer of energy after the United States and third largest importer of oil. About 70% of China's energy needs are supplied by coal, which it mines in greater quantity than any other nation. A major effort is underway to develop vast offshore oil fields and to harness the hydroelectric potential of China's rivers. The Three Gorges chain of dams on the Yangzi is the largest project of its kind ever undertaken. Yet China's dependence on coal will continue for decades, greatly contributing to pollution and global warming.

INDUSTRY

China's economy has been growing by 9% annually for nearly thirty years. The PRC is the world's leader in the production of coal, steel, aluminum, and concrete and among the leaders in the production of uranium, tungsten, tin, and chemical fertilizers. Chinese factories produce two-thirds of the world's copiers, microwave ovens, DVD players, shoes, and toys. Other major industries include machinery, armaments, and textiles. Many government-controlled factories have been closed or "spun-off" as privately owned factories. The realignment of much of China's industrial base has caused layoffs and unemployment, estimated at 8–10% in urban areas. Still, job mobility has greatly increased, and the rapid expansion of free enterprise in China has created jobs by the tens of millions.

Heavy industry is hampered by aging equipment and poor working conditions. Worker safety is too often ignored in favor of increased production. Miners, construction crews, and workers in such heavy industries as steel-making have particularly dirty, hard, and dangerous jobs. Workers in many light industries, such as clothing and pottery manufacturing, labor in hot, stuffy, and poorly lit factories. The workweek is long, often ten hours a day, five and a half or six days a week. Thousands of new factories have been built in recent years, but China is so vast that it will take years, perhaps decades, to equip all of Chinese industry with modern tools and healthy working conditions.

Etching metalwork

FOREIGN TRADE

After the United States and Germany, China is the world's largest trading nation. Exports to the United States have grown 1,600% in the last fifteen years. Of Wal-Mart's 6,000 major suppliers, 5,000 are in China. China has seen its own imports grow by 415% since 1991.

Chinese banks are the world's second largest holders of foreign exchange reserves, $1.3 trillion. China's willingness to buy treasury bonds underwrites much of the United States budget deficit. A downturn in China's volatile stock market immediately causes jitters in financial capitals around the world.

Nearly every economist recognizes that an economic collapse in China would cause a worldwide depression.

AGRICULTURE

About 50% of China's workforce is still employed in agriculture. China is among the world's leaders in the production of rice, wheat, potatoes, millet, barley, peanuts, sorghum, pork, soybeans, tobacco, tea, and cotton.

Age-old farming methods and tools are still common in China. Many peasant families still use wooden plows, hoes, rakes, barrels, and wheelbarrows; woven baskets, mats, and fences; and pottery jars of every size and description. Horses, donkeys, and water buffalo are still common. However, the introduction of modern technology is rapidly changing rural China. Today more families and family groups can afford tractors and other modern tools. Chemical fertilizers, pesticides and herbicides, and better seed have produced large increases in crop yields.

In the early years of reform, rural incomes skyrocketed, but they have stagnated in recent years. There is an excess of labor available, causing widespread unemployment and underemployment. An estimated 100 million rural workers seek jobs in urban areas for at least part of the year. The government is pushing massive investment in building rural factories to increase employment opportunities in the countryside. Eventually, the government hopes to slow or even reverse the migration from countryside to overcrowded cities through the development of rural manufacturing centers of 50,000 to 100,000 people.

Beijing Capital International Airport

TRANSPORTATION

The economic expansion since 1978 would have been impossible without the government's emphasis on building a modern transportation system. Primitive by Western standards a generation ago, China's highway system today measures some 80,600 miles (130,000 km), almost equivalent to that of the United States. Half of the secondary road system is unpaved, but the government continues to invest huge sums in the development of China's roadways. Today 13.3 billion tons (72.4%) of freight moves by road. Private vehicle ownership still makes up only a small percentage of the traffic, but that too is changing as more and more Chinese families achieve incomes that allow the purchase of a car.

Railroads handle more human and freight transportation per mile in China than any railroad system in the world with the exception of even more densely populated India. In 2005, China had some 46,000 miles (74,000 km) of track moving over a billion passengers and 2.7 billion tons (14.6%) of freight. The government has established three massive public corporations to handle freight and passenger transportation with the goal of increasing track length to 56,000 miles (90,000 km) by 2010.

China's 75,000 miles (121,000 km) of inland waterways include 5,800 rivers and 5,100 inland ports. Incorporated in this system is an incredible system of canals, some more than 2,000 years old. One quarter of the inland waterways can handle oceangoing ships. Some 400 million passengers and 2.1 billion tons (11.4%) of freight move by inland waterways. China's leaders believe that the waterways could move many times that volume of traffic and have sought development funds from Western investors and the World Bank.

By Western standards, China's air transportation network still lags, but development is making strides as tourism increases and more Chinese find themselves able to afford airline fares. Today, 129 airports have regularly scheduled flights. The amount of cargo moved by air is still insignificant compared to other means, but that too will change as modern business conditions demand more timely deliveries.

LIVING STANDARDS

In the twenty-five years from 1981 to 2006, economic reform in China lifted 350 million people out of poverty, quadrupled per capita income, and lowered the poverty rate from 53% to 8%. But the boom is not equally shared. While some Chinese have grown rich, many times more—an estimated 100–150 million—still live on less than $1 per day.

The average Chinese income ($2,000 in 2006) is low by Western standards but rising. Under the commune system established by Mao in 1957, most families owned little more than their clothing, bedding, cooking pots, a few tools, and two or three prized possessions. In the early years of economic reform in the 1980's, Chinese saved for the "four acquisitions": a wristwatch, a bicycle, a sewing machine, and a radio. As China thrived in the early 1990's, the list evolved into "the eight bigs": an electric fan, a motorcycle, a refrigerator, a suite of furniture, a washing machine, a camera, a stereo, and a color television.

**Although new technology powers much of Chinese industry,
huge amounts of work are still performed by muscle and stamina.**

As the nation approached the turn of the millennium, income disparities increased. Rural incomes stagnated. Coastal cities thrived while inland cities lagged behind. Economic growth benefited people with education and professional or management jobs more than workers and peasants. The rise of a prosperous middle class is one the striking developments of economic reform. Under the Maoist version of communism, the middle class—or the bourgeoisie—was stripped of its wealth and privileges. But the economic reformers have promoted its resurgence, recognizing that historically the middle class has driven economic development. It is, however, a dangerous game for the Communist Party since history also teaches that a strong middle class is the principal force in democratic change.

EDUCATION

Chinese family traditions are strong, and Chinese adults are doting parents and grandparents. Since most young adults work, a child is often left in the care of a grandparent living in the home. If this arrangement is not possible, the child is usually placed in a child-care facility connected with his or her school. Because of the length of the long Chinese workweek, some children see their parents only on weekends.

Before the Communist government came to power in 1949, 80% of the people were illiterate. The government has pushed a massive program of adult and child education into the far corners of the country. Today, the government claims, over 90% of the people can read and write. Other estimates put the literacy level significantly lower.

Chinese children average nine years in school. Kindergartens accept children as young as three, and almost all Chinese children begin school by age five. Courses are similar to those in schools the world over, with a particular emphasis on citizenship and learning to work together. Yearly examinations begin in elementary school. After sixth grade, the more able students enter an academic secondary school while the rest begin vocational programs that include part-time work outside of school. The most able students focus on winning government scholarships that will allow them to attend vocational colleges or academic universities. Local and provincial governments bear most of the cost of primary and secondary education. In poorer areas of the country, there is a shortage of good facilities, modern textbooks, and trained staff.

Conditions are crowded in China's large university system, and most students have only enough money for the basic necessities. As they have for centuries, Chinese parents sacrifice to make a college education possible for their children. A principal element of traditional Chinese culture is a huge respect for higher education. From the time the ancient scholar-mandarins first ruled China in the name of the emperor, a higher education brought great pride to families and both privileges and responsibilities to the individual. In the first thirty years of the People's Republic, intellectuals were often attacked as "revisionists," "capitalist-roaders," or worse. Today, however, a new generation of engineers, managers, economists, and similar "technocrats" are leading China's economic rebirth. In 1982, only 2.4% of high school students passed college entrance exams. By 2002, the figure had jumped to 50%.

A rural schoolhouse

DIET

The daily diet is plain. In the South, people eat a great deal of rice—five or six bowls a day. Noodles are the staple in the North. The main meal of the day—at noon in the countryside and at evening in the city—includes vegetables, soup, rice or noodles, and a small amount of pork, chicken, duck, or fish. Meat and vegetables are cut into tiny pieces, wasting nothing that can be eaten, and steamed or stir-fried in a wok. In various parts of the country, soy sauce, vinegar, garlic, mustard, ginger, hot peppers, and scallions are used to add flavor to the dishes. Banquets of a dozen or more courses mark special occasions, and their memory is savored for months afterward.

Green tea, the national drink, is consumed in steaming quantities even on the hottest days. (Cultural tradition prizes moderation and few Chinese abuse alcohol or drugs. Unfortunately, tobacco addiction is commonplace.) For the many families that don't have refrigerators, shopping is a daily chore. The government no longer rations basic foodstuffs but continues to maintain price controls on some basic commodities. The danger of famine—the age-old curse of China—has receded in recent years, but the government admits that malnutrition remains a problem in poorer parts of the country.

Crabs for sale in a free market

MEDICAL CARE

The quality of medical care in China varies widely. Big cities boast world-class hospitals and clinics, but in rural areas the care falls off rapidly. In Mao's China, the government provided free medical care to everyone. The system was awkward and the care often of low quality. The reformers have attempted to improve the system by allowing doctors and medical facilities to charge patients. The results have been disappointing. China has more and better doctors and facilities than ever before, but many people cannot afford treatment. Waiting times are long, particularly for those without political influence or money enough for bribes.

By necessity or preference, many people resort to home remedies or treatment by traditional practitioners. About a third of China's doctors practice Western medicine while the rest use traditional healing methods. The most famous traditional method is acupuncture. Ancient belief describes a system where the life force, called *T'chi*, flows through the body along fourteen paths. If the *T'chi* is disturbed, the loss of balance between its negative side, the *Yin*, and its positive side, the *Yang*, causes illness. Inserting thin needles into several of the 800 acupuncture points on the body restores the balance and cures the patient. Dismissed as superstition in the West for centuries, acupuncture has gained respect in recent years, particularly for the treatment of pain. Modern research indicates that the needles affect the body's nerve paths, blocking feeling from reaching the brain.

**Herbs, many with medicinal
uses, for sale in a free market**

Because of crowded conditions and the proximity of domestic animals to humans, China has long been an incubator of viruses. Annually, scientists rush to identify the latest strain of influenza emerging from China. Diseases such as SARS and bird flu have set off worldwide health alerts. During the SARS crisis in 2003, China's leaders welcomed help from international agencies for the first time. The policy has continued, and China now cooperates fully with the World Health Organization, United Nations AIDS Project, and numerous foreign institutions and organizations.

As a percentage of population, the incidence of HIV/AIDS in China is low by world standards. China reported its first AIDS case in 1985. Government officials demonstrated little concern over the next decade, dismissing HIV/AIDS as the "loving capitalism disease." But an epidemic exploded in the mid-1990's, driven mainly by a rapid increase in intravenous drug use. By 1998, every province had reported HIV/AIDS cases and the national total had reached 100,000. Admitting at last that China had a major problem, the government launched a national education effort. In the decade since, the government has taken strong action to control both the causes and effects of HIV/AIDS. In 2006, the Ministry of Health estimated that 650,000 people were living with HIV/AIDS. Outside experts estimated the true figure at two to three times that number. Predictions for the future vary widely. The government hopes to keep the number below 1.5 million. Some outside experts fear that 10 to 15 million people could be infected by 2010.

CRIME

Unfortunately, crime is on the rise in today's China. A large migrant population of seasonal laborers, layoffs, increasing income disparities, and other economic and social problems have led to an increase in prostitution, drug use, and petty crime. A significant number of businessmen and public officials have been convicted of corruption, bribery, and unfair labor practices. Organized crime has reappeared, particularly in some of the major cities.

A passerby examines wanted posters.

HOUSING AND PRIVACY

Many of China's cities have a severe housing shortage. In urban areas three generations may share an apartment the size of an American living room. A recently married couple may live for years with relatives before being able to afford an apartment of their own. Many lower income residents resent losing their homes to luxury housing developments they cannot afford.

Outside the major cities, many homes still lack electricity and running water. Kerosene lamps provide light, and water is drawn from a communal tap or pump. Some of the more modern rural districts have long rows of single-story apartments. Elsewhere, peasants have individual homes with two or three small rooms. The walls of most homes are built of mud bricks, and the few windows are often covered with paper rather than glass. In the North, where the winters are cold, the brick beds are heated from below with pipes running from the stove. These traditional homes are gradually being replaced by more modern housing as rural families enjoy a higher standard of living under reform.

Commune housing

RELIGION

In Mao's China, religious practice was discouraged as a remnant of an imperialist and capitalist past. The government closed churches, mosques, temples, and monasteries and ordered priests, ministers, monks, and nuns to take jobs in the workforce. Since 1978, the reformers have set aside many of these restrictions and allowed the reopening of some religious buildings. The reformers permit the people to celebrate traditional festivals abolished or renamed under Mao. Today, the mid-autumn festival is once again the Moon Goddess festival.

Monk lighting incense

Mao dismissed ancestor veneration as another relic of China's past that must be discarded. Communist authorities forbade family altars to ancestors and ordered the plowing of family graveyards to gain more farmland, a policy psychologically devastating for traditional Chinese. Most of those graveyards remain under cultivation today, but the practice of ancestor veneration is no longer forbidden.

The government tends to underestimate the number of people who actively practice religious faiths. It estimates that there are 5 million Catholics, 15 million Protestants, 20 million Muslims, 100 million Buddhists, and a large but uncounted number of Daoists. The actual numbers are probably much higher. A recent Beijing University study found that 31% of

Chinese sixteen years and older follow some form of religious practice, putting the total number of believers at some 400 million.

The Communist government remains deeply suspicious of religion, strictly forbidding any mixing of religion and politics. In recent years, the government has suppressed the Falun Gong movement, an action protested by Amnesty International and numerous religious leaders outside China.

Falun Gong was founded in 1992 by Li Hongzhi, a charismatic store clerk who claimed to have studied Buddhism under great masters. The group's beliefs are a mixture Buddhist and Daoist meditation practices and Li Hongzhi's personal claims to know the past and the future. The movement grew rapidly in the 1990's, attracting the government's concern. In early 1999, the government banned several Falun Gong publications for refusing government oversight. Several thousand Falun Gong protested in Beijing, briefly blocking the car of President Jiang Zemin. Already worried that Falun Gong was becoming a messianic movement dedicated to a single man, the government struck back hard. It outlawed Falun Gong and arrested tens of thousands of followers, sending some to labor camps for as long as three years. Lecturing abroad at the time of the suppression, Li Hongzhi settled in the United States.

A PHILOSOPHY OF ETHICS

The vast majority of Chinese before the revolution adhered to the ancient philosophy of Confucianism. The wise man Confucius (551–479 B.C.) outlined a philosophy for maintaining social order based on rules of mutual respect and ethical dealings. Never a religion, Confucianism nevertheless fit well with the age-old Chinese reverence for ancestors. Hence the inaccurate portrayal in older Western texts of Confucianism as "ancestor worship." For the Chinese, however, Confucianism remained a philosophy of "right conduct."

For decades after the revolution, the Communists denounced Confucianism as a relic of the "Old China." In order for the Chinese people to achieve the communal society envisioned by Mao, they must abandon the old rules outlined by the ancient sage. But the task of rooting out Confucianism proved too much even for Mao, and Confucian ethics and traditions remained very much a part of the Chinese character. Today, the reformers speak of taking the best from both communism and Confucianism in the push to modernize China. The government has announced plans to establish 500 Confucian institutes by 2010.

The Great Hall of the People

THE COMMUNIST PARTY

The Chinese Communist Party (CCP) dominates the People's Republic. The Party has about 70 million members. Membership is granted only to those citizens who show particular knowledge of and loyalty to Marxist-Leninism, Mao Zedong Thought, and Deng Xiaoping Theory.

The National Congress of the CCP meets every five years to debate Party policy. In the interim, a select committee, called the Politburo, determines and administers Party policy. Within this committee, the Standing Committee exerts day-to-day authority, electing from its members the principal administrator of Party affairs, the general secretary.

Members of the CCP hold virtually all major posts at all levels of government from local to national. Other parties do exist, but they are small and only permitted to give China the appearance of a multiparty state.

THE STATE STRUCTURE

According to the constitution of the PRC, ultimate power resides in the National People's Congress (NPC), which meets for two weeks annually. Long a rubber stamp for decisions made by senior leadership, its members have become more vocal and assertive in recent years. The NPC elects the president of the PRC, the president of the Supreme People's Court, and the Standing Committee of the NPC, which exerts the NPC's authority when the Congress is not in session.

The president is expected to set general policy for the PRC. He has the right to declare war and to conduct foreign affairs. He appoints the State Council and its senior member, the premier, to administer the many state ministries.

The State structure outlined in China's constitution seems to guarantee a large amount of power to the people. In reality, power resides in the hands of, at most, two- or three-dozen individuals, most of whom hold high positions in both the CCP and the State structure. The general secretary of the CCP is, almost always, also the president. (In recent years, the title president has taken precedence over general secretary, a reflection of the reformers' preference for emphasizing State over Party titles.) Members of the Politburo fill many of the State Council seats. The premier is always a member of the Politburo Standing Committee. These individuals make deals and alliances that allow them to push their policies and candidates for positions in the government.

China's provinces, independent municipalities, and special autonomous regions have governmental structures very similar to the national government's. Again, the CCP dominates. Successful governors and provincial Party chairmen are frequently elevated to senior positions in the national government to provide new blood and fresh ideas. Some provinces have become wealthy in the era of reform, giving their governors considerable leverage in negotiating with the national government. Often strapped for cash, the central government must now negotiate with provincial governments it once dominated.

Provinces are subdivided into prefectures made up of several counties. Counties are subdivided into townships (or municipalities), and townships into villages. Since the mid-1990's, the central government has expanded village and township elections. However, the CCP has ceded little real power and, despite lip service to the development of democracy, appears to have little intention of doing so.

THE PEOPLE'S LIBERATION ARMY

The People's Liberation Army (PLA) is the world's largest military force. Increasingly professional and well equipped, it represents a worrisome force to the West. Although constitutionally subordinate to the government, the PLA has always maintained a strong sense of independence in government and Party debates. (The Party has its own representatives in the military through a system of political commissars.) Senior officers serve on the State Military Commission. The chairmanship is a position of great power, and is usually sought by the President. However, if he is not elected by the members, the winning candidate may become a serious rival. (Deng Xiaoping, the principal architect of the reform movement after the death of Mao in 1976, allowed others to take the top positions in the government and Party, maintaining his influence from a position as chairman of the State and CCP military commissions.)

SU-27 Flanker fighter

In 1971, General Lin Biao, the defense minister and Mao's designated successor, allegedly tried to orchestrate a military coup and Mao's assassination. The plot failed because of the loyalty of most of the high command to Mao and Premier Zhou Enlai (1899–1976). However, there remains the potential danger that the PLA could take over the government in a time of national crisis.

COOPERATION AND CONFORMITY

Privacy is a great luxury in much of China. In both city and rural district, several families may share a bathroom and a kitchen. Only through cooperation and patience can people accomplish routine chores. Arguments in courtyard and street are community affairs, with neighbors gathering to listen and to mediate. Considering the crowded conditions, it is remarkable that life goes on so smoothly.

Relatives, neighbors, schoolmates, or fellow workers will correct an individual who violates social standards. This pressure is usually enough to correct the problem. If it isn't, local authorities will step in, perhaps forcing the nonconformist to submit to "public criticism" during a community or factory meeting.

Chinese tradition prizes cooperation and conformity to accepted social standards. China simply does not have room for over 1.3 billion "rugged individualists." A good citizen keeps his individuality within tight limits, and a stubborn nonconformist is usually viewed as a troublemaker. A phrase for the Chinese attitude entered English during World War II: gung ho—work together.

Beijing

A BOOMING ECONOMY

Economic figures give testament to China's success in the era of reform that began when Deng Xiaoping and the pragmatists took charge of the government in 1978. Today, some 70% of China's gross national product (GDP) is produced by the private sector. Between 1978 and January 2006, China's GDP increased 3,900% from 362.4 billion rimimbi to 14,147.7 billion. Grain output increased from 304.8 million tons in 1978 to 469.5 million by 2004. Foreign exchange reserves grew from $1.6 billion in 1978 to $1.3 trillion by mid-2007.

China is America's third largest trading partner after Canada and Mexico. In turn, the United States is China's second largest trading partner, following the 25-nation European Union. In 2005, the United States imported $243 billion in Chinese goods while exporting $42 billion in goods. Though

American exports to China are growing at a healthy rate (157% between 2000 and 2005) the $201 billion deficit worries American economists and government leaders.

Two-thirds of China's exports are such labor-intensive products as toys, furniture, shoes, fabric items, and appliances. Chinese companies import electronic parts made elsewhere, assembling them into finished products (e.g. copiers and DVD players) for export. Some 85% of China's imports are machinery, sophisticated electronics, agricultural products, and energy.

CHINA'S CENTURY?

The Chinese people have made extraordinary progress, creating talk that the 21st century may be "China's Century." Already one of the world's leading manufacturing and exporting countries, China may have only begun to demonstrate the potential of its economy. In a period when the United States has lost respect and status in the world because of its involvement in Iraq, many countries are looking to China to provide new leadership. Still, China has huge problems it must deal with in the near future or risk the loss of all the successes and hopes of recent years. To understand how China arrived at this critical time in its long and troubled history, we must look far back into China's past.

Near the headwaters of the Yellow River

Chapter 2
The First Chinese

The evidence of humans in China dates back some 50,000 years. These ancestors of today's Chinese were Ice Age hunters and gatherers. They lived in small bands and migrated with the seasons in search of animals and ripening wild fruits and vegetables. Like Stone Age peoples everywhere, they feasted in times of plenty and went hungry in lean seasons.

The search for more reliable sources of food led to the development of primitive agriculture between 7,000 and 8,000 years ago. Some of the bands began reseeding wild crops and domesticating small animals. As they devoted more of their time to farming, they spent less time wandering. They established permanent villages and joined other bands in larger tribal organizations. The Wei and Yellow River valleys of north-central China proved especially adaptable to this new way of life and became the cradle of Chinese civilization.

Chinese junk on the Yangtze:
a design more than 2,000 years old

The Yellow Emperor

The success of agriculture produced a rapidly increasing population and the need for a stronger governmental system to keep peace and to promote cooperation. Chinese tradition says that a ruler named Huang Di (the Yellow Emperor) united the tribes of north-central China about 2500 B.C. Huang Di and his wise counselors are credited with building the first cities, writing a code of laws, introducing public and religious ceremonies, and inventing the compass, the calendar, and the written language. Although no doubt embellished in the retelling, the stories of Huang Di's reign reveal an early yearning by the Chinese people for unity and stable government.

Sometime between 2000 and 1950 B.C., a heroic figure named the Emperor Yu answered that yearning by founding China's first ruling dynasty, the Xia. For nearly 4,000 years, China would be ruled by emperors who, on their death, handed over power to a chosen son or other close relative. Some of the dynasties sputtered and died in a few decades, others lasted for centuries.

Most of the history of the Xia dynasty, even its very existence, is clouded by myth. But we do know that in this period the people in the Yellow River basin built massive flood-control dikes, developed silk weaving, began making fine pottery, adopted the use of bronze tools, and added several thousand characters to the written language.

WRITTEN HISTORY BEGINS

The cloud of myth begins to lift with the Shang dynasty, the first dynasty to leave written records. The Shang came to power somewhere between 1766

B.C. and 1576 B.C. The new dynasty established a class structure with a ruling class of hereditary nobles just below the emperor, an administrative class to maintain detailed records, and an artisan class to make beautiful possessions for the ruling classes. The majority of the people farmed the land, supporting the upper classes with their labor and taxes. The Shang rulers constructed cities surrounded by massive walls and built fine homes and palaces. Pottery and tool making, weaving, and writing became highly developed arts. Shang craftsmen cast bronze statues with techniques unequaled in Europe for another 2,500 years. Shang emperors were buried in large tombs with hoards of beautiful possessions and scores of human and animal sacrifices.

Shang bronze

As was to happen over and over again in Chinese history, the Shang dynasty eventually lost energy and efficiency. The peasants and slaves at the lowest levels of society became resentful of the cruelty and extravagance of the rulers. Wars and official corruption drained the emperor's treasury. About 1026 B.C. the nobility of the state of Zhou overthrew the Shang. According to legend, the last Shang emperor threw himself into the flames of his burning palace.

The Zhou became the longest ruling dynasty in Chinese history, lasting until 256 B.C. Chinese history and legend credit Ji Dan, the Duke of Zhou, with establishing the ruling principles that would enable the dynasty to last eight centuries. A man of awesome and varied talents, the Duke of Zhou was the principle advisor to his older brother, the King of Wu, during the rebellion against the Shang and the king's brief reign as the first Zhou emperor. The Duke of Zhou then became regent for his brother's young son, consolidating the rule of the dynasty and selflessly handing over power when his nephew, Cheng Wang, came of age. Cheng Wang enjoyed a happy reign of thirty-seven years thanks to his own outstanding character and the advice of his uncle. So esteemed would the duke's memory become that even today a Chinese leader can receive no greater praise than to be compared to the Duke of Zhou.

THE MANDATE OF HEAVEN

Both a statesman and a philosopher, the Duke of Zhou incorporated ethics and religion into the ruling principles of the dynasty. Thousands of years before, China's Stone Age peoples had developed a folk religion that included hundreds of gods. Seasons, the sun and the moon, natural phenomena such as rain and wind, and geographical features such as a river or a mountain could each have a god. No particular god was more true than another, all existing as part of the spiritual world. Some of the more prominent gods were celebrated at annual festivals that often corresponded with stages in the cycle of the farming year. A festival for the Sun was celebrated in the spring as the planting season began; the Moon Goddess festival occurred at harvest time in mid-autumn. Eventually, China's first astronomers would determine the dates of these festivals by careful lunar observations.

Veneration of ancestors became part of traditional Chinese religion. Most Chinese adopted the practice of making prayers and small offerings to the spirits of departed ancestors. However, assigning the label "ancestor worship" to these practices is a mistake. The ancient Chinese believed that the spirits of the departed still resided in the world at least some of the time. They offered their prayers and gifts to express love and good wishes to the departed and to ask for their help in overcoming problems. Many later Chinese would come to see the practice not so much as an attempt to influence the spirits but as an opportunity to remind the living of family traditions and to reflect on the example of respected ancestors.

In the second millennium B.C., the concept of Heaven became central to Chinese religion. In some uses Heaven was another name for an all-powerful creator god, Shangdi. However, Shangdi was a rather remote figure, and most Chinese devoted more time to venerating lesser and more accessible gods. Despite the claims of some Christian missionaries many centuries later, Shangdi and the Christian God were not interchangeable figures. The vast majority of Chinese remained emphatically pantheistic, rejecting the monotheistic belief in a single god. Western Christianity never gained a large following in China because of its insistence on the worship of a single God to the exclusion of all others. Likewise, Islam, with its monotheistic belief in Allah, would never thrive among the Han majority.

The concept of Heaven had a greater political and cultural importance as representing not a single personified god but a heavenly realm of pure harmony. As a force Heaven could have great influence on the affairs of human beings. Correct behavior by the people and their rulers brought the approval of Heaven and a time of peace, good crops, and social harmony. Incorrect behavior brought war, floods, famine, and revolt.

The Duke of Zhou introduced the concept that dynasties ruled with the Mandate of Heaven. He wrote that the later Shang emperors had ruled poorly, angering Heaven, and losing the Mandate. Hence, the Zhou were justified in overthrowing the Shang and assuming the Mandate of Heaven as the new dynasty.

As the reigning "Son of Heaven," an emperor needed to maintain the approval of Heaven. The Zhou and later dynasties built temples, established a priesthood, and developed ceremonies of homage to Heaven. Until the 20th century, the worship of Heaven would serve as the formal state religion. Individually, the Chinese enjoyed almost complete religious freedom to venerate what gods they chose in whatever manner they chose. Emperors, however, were under strict obligation to render homage to Heaven in the name of all the people.

THE FEUDAL SYSTEM

The Zhou emperors established a feudal system, giving vast estates (or fiefdoms) to princes and nobles, who in turn contributed money, goods, soldiers, and laborers to the emperor. Aggressive princes extended China's borders outward into lands inhabited by "barbarian" peoples. Some of these powerful princes became virtually independent. Although the Zhou dynasty lasted for eight centuries, it often ruled in name only outside its capital in the Wei River valley.

Throughout the Zhou dynasty, the Chinese population grew rapidly as more and more land came under cultivation. Cities flourished, iron tools replaced bronze, crafts were refined to a high level, and trade spread far and wide. The late Zhou period produced a surge of interest in education, poetry, literature, and philosophy. Scholars and philosophers gained great esteem in Chinese society.

THE SEARCH FOR ANSWERS

The squabbles and ambitions of the feudal princes and petty kings in the late Zhou period worked against the welfare of the majority of Chinese. Reacting to the instability, scholar-philosophers developed philosophies for organizing a just and orderly society.

Laozi   **Confucius**

Daoism (Taoism) was based on the teachings of Laozi, a holy man who lived in the sixth century B.C. Daoists believed in putting aside earthly ambition and desire to seek harmony with the forces of nature. The ideal Daoist society would need few rules, since people living in harmony with nature would naturally live in harmony with each other. A kindly emperor would protect the people from want and strong passions with a minimum number of rules. Over the centuries, Daoism developed into a religion with many ceremonies, gods, and mystical practices.

The scholar and teacher Confucius (551?–479? B.C.) wrestled with the problem of devising a system for a just and harmonious society. Confucius looked to the writings and character of the Duke of Zhou for inspiration. His theory emphasized the importance of education, individual self-discipline, and strict obedience to a detailed code of conduct. Starting with the Chinese family, Confucius laid out rules of address and behavior for each member.

Extending outward, the same rules gave everyone at every layer of Chinese society a code of behavior. In the ideal Confucian society, everyone from the emperor to the poorest peasant would know his or her place and behave accordingly. Society would become stable and harmonious for all time.

The Legalists made up the third school of thought. Unlike the followers of Confucius, who wanted to order society from the family outward, the Legalists wanted to impose order from the top down. They believed that the emperor should enact detailed and strict laws to cover nearly all aspects of behavior. Confronted with the prospect of harsh and certain punishment for disobedience, people would behave properly.

As different as they seem, Daoism, Confucianism, and Legalism each found a place in the Chinese view of the world. The Chinese celebrated their reverence for the natural world with Daoism, ordered family and social ethics according to Confucianism, and—for the most part—accepted Legalism's advice that a multitude of laws were needed to regulate society.

CHINA IS UNITED

The early Legalists found champions in the aggressive rulers of the Qin kingdom in the Wei River Valley. By the 3rd century B.C., Chinese civilization had spread over much of what is today eastern China. This vast and, by the standards of the time, heavily populated area was divided among seven feudal kings who paid little attention to the emperor of the decaying Zhou dynasty.

About 328 B.C., the Qin set out to conquer the rest of China. The wars lasted more than a century and cost millions of lives. Without a strong dynasty to unite them against the Qin, the other six Zhou kingdoms fell one by one. In 246 B.C., the reigning king of Qin—a young man barely in his teens—declared himself Shi Huangdi, "the first emperor." By 221 B.C., he had conquered the last of his rivals and united China into a single centralized state.

Brilliant, cruel, greedy, and daring, Shi Huangdi (c.259–209 B.C.) changed China for all time. As his armies marched out to conquer new territories, Shi Huangdi set about bringing order to his vast empire. On the advice of his Legalist ministers, he abolished the old feudal system and divided China into provinces under governors serving at his pleasure. Treachery, corruption, or poor performance by any official brought quick removal and, probably, execution.

Shi Huangdi

Shi Huangdi built a dazzling new capital near Xi'an on the Yellow River. His palaces, shrines, gardens, roads, pools, and paths covered some twenty-five square miles (65 sq. km). Luxury cost money and the emperor's Legalist advisors furiously composed new taxes to go along with laws covering nearly every aspect of Chinese life. Many of Shi Huangdi's reforms were of great benefit to the people. He decreed that all carts must have the same axle width so that they could all travel easily along the empire's deeply rutted roads. He introduced a uniform system of weights and measures, standardized the empire's coinage, and issued a set of standard written characters.

Shi Huangdi stamped out opposition with ruthless efficiency. Anyone who criticized him or his Legalist advisers risked instant execution. He ordered the burning of all books that might threaten his new order—a tragic act that destroyed much of China's written history, philosophy, poetry, and literature. He forbade any discussion of the past, declaring that Chinese history was to begin with the Qin dynasty and its first emperor.

THE GREAT WALL

Shi Huangdi worried about invasion by the fierce tribes that wandered the forests and steppes beyond the northern border of his domain. He decided to construct a barrier against their raids on his settled, peaceable subjects. He connected a series of older walls to form a huge new wall. The Great Wall of China remains the largest construction project in history. Forty feet (12 m) high in places and wide enough for five horses to gallop abreast, it stretches some 1,500 miles (2,400 km) across northern China. Counting bends, dips, and branching walls, its total length exceeds 3,700 miles (5,960 km). Chinese tradition says that it took thirty years to complete and cost "a life for every stone."

Shi Huangdi died in 209 B.C. and was buried outside Xi'an in a magnificent underground tomb the size of a small city. (Although archaeologists have explored only a very small portion of Shi Huangdi's tomb, they have already uncovered an army of larger than life-size clay soldiers and horses.) Without its strong ruler, the Qin dynasty crumbled. Enraged by the brutality and greed of the dynasty, peasants and nobles joined forces to defeat the Qin armies. The victorious nobles attempted to restore the feudal system, but the common people resisted a return to the bad old days. In 202 B.C. the great peasant leader Liu Bang defeated the last of his opponents to unite China under a new dynasty built on the ruins of the Qin. Despite its short life, the Qin dynasty had changed China in extraordinary ways. The political system established by Shi Huangdi would survive until the 20th century.

The Great Wall

Chapter 3
Emperors, Dynasties, and Mandarins

In 202 B.C., Liu Bang became the first emperor of the Han dynasty. Although a person of little education, he was a shrewd ruler. He awarded land to his generals and those nobles who had sided with him, but he kept their fiefdoms small and weak by surrounding them with large provinces under the control of royal governors.

The emperors who followed Liu Bang carefully chipped away at the power of the nobles. In 144 B.C., the Emperor Xiao Jing decreed that every lord must will his lands in equal parts to all his sons, rather than leaving the entire fiefdom to the eldest—a practice called primogeniture. This clever decree so divided the wealth of the nobility that within two or three generations they became little more than minor landlords unable to threaten the power of the emperor.

The Han emperors courted the loyalty of the scholar class. Confucian scholars had originally opposed the concentration of power in the hands of a central government (the policy of the Legalists). But the Han emperors wooed them with rich appointments, prestige, and a willingness to listen. Soon the Confucian scholars became the imperial system's strongest backers.

Han dynasty coin

THE MANDARINS
The Han emperors recruited the governing officials of the empire from the scholar class. Candidates spent long years studying the Confucian texts to learn the principles of good government and harmonious society. Usually in their late twenties or early thirties, candidates felt ready to tackle the rigorous government examinations. Locked in tiny cubicles for days on end, some

candidates went mad or committed suicide. Others did so poorly that they were given only minor positions as clerks and tax collectors. But those who emerged with high scores could look forward to careers of wealth and power.

**19th century painting showing
generations of a mandarin family**

A scholar who achieved one of the nine highest levels in the examinations could adopt the dress and title of a mandarin. The mandarins were a remarkable class of scholar-officials. Unlike any other ruling class in the world, they held their positions not because of inherited wealth or blood ties to the royal family but because of their intelligence and education. In theory, a young man from the lowest class could become a mandarin if he had the brains and energy to master the knowledge needed to pass the examinations. Some succeeded, but the expense of getting the necessary education kept most young men—no matter how bright—out of the mandarin class.

The mandarins became indispensable to the day-to-day governing of the vast empire. Although dynasties rose and fell, the mandarins maintained their power for 2,000 years.

Imperial examination cubicles

THE IMPERIAL HOUSEHOLD

Intelligent and energetic emperors kept a careful watch on the great web of administration extending from the imperial court to the smallest and most distant village in the land. Emperors spent their lives surrounded with innumerable luxuries and armies of servants. Yet the constant work of reading and signing documents, consulting with senior ministers, and performing state and religious ceremonies taxed an emperor's stamina. Intrigue and jealousy plagued the court, and the constant danger of assassination haunted their lives.

Emperors had as many as twenty or thirty wives and many more concubines. The women's apartments were a center of intrigue as wives and concubines competed to gain the emperor's favor. Although the first wife might expect her eldest son to become the next "son of Heaven," his position was by no means assured as other wives tried to bring their sons' virtues to the emperor's attention. Women who gained high favor could persuade an emperor to appoint their fathers, uncles, brothers, and nephews to positions as ministers and generals. Weak or child emperors often became mere figureheads controlled by powerful families.

**Admiral Zheng He, a powerful eunuch,
explored the Indian Ocean in the early 1400's.**

A class of court servants, called eunuchs, conspired with or against the women and their families. Castrated as boys to deprive them of any sexual interest in women, the eunuchs guarded the harem and waited on the emperor. Through their daily contact with the imperial family, some eunuchs gained great influence and high positions in the government. Quite naturally, they became the enemies of the senior mandarins who had qualified for positions through the examination system.

THE CLASS SYSTEM

Traditional Chinese society was organized rather like a spider's web, with the emperor and his family at the center and the rest of the people occupying bands radiating outward in ever-widening circles. The band nearest the center was occupied by the senior mandarins and their competitors for influence: the court eunuchs and the relatives of wives or concubines who enjoyed the emperor's favor. Lesser mandarins occupied the next band outward, while non-mandarin officials (tax collectors, clerks, inspectors, teachers, and the like) occupied the rays of the web extending to its outer extremities, where some minor officials were very poor.

The first band beyond the inner government circles was occupied by wealthy landlords, merchants, manufacturers, shipowners, and mine operators, whose riches gave them considerable influence. Rich peasant farmers, who rented most of their land to others or hired laborers to work it for them, occupied the next band. They lived comfortable lives and exerted considerable political influence on the local level. Artisans, craft workers, shopkeepers, junior army officers, doctors, moneylenders, monks, nuns, and the practitioners of innumerable other trades lived on the next band, where riches were much less abundant.

The vast majority of the Chinese people occupied the wide middle bands. First came the so-called "middle" peasants, who owned all or most of their land, perhaps renting a few extra acres from a wealthy landlord. Next came the poor peasants, who had to rent almost all their land or work on the farms of others. All told, nine out of ten Chinese lived on these two wide bands far from the wealth and power concentrated in the narrow rings close to the center. The poor peasants lived hard lives of grinding labor in all seasons, forever at the mercy of the weather, bandits, and the rich landlords who owned most of the land. When crops failed, millions of peasants starved, and even in good times extreme thrift was necessary for the vast majority of Chinese.

Common soldiers and sailors (held in low esteem in Chinese society and paid little), laborers, peddlers, rickshaw pullers, and other landless workers occupied the next to the last band. On the outermost band lived the humblest citizens of all: butchers, hide tanners, prostitutes, dung collectors, wandering actors and singers, and the practitioners of other spurned or "unclean" occupations. Outside the web entirely were the castoffs of society: beggars, lepers, pickpockets, thieves, and bandits.

THE MIDDLE KINGDOM

The Chinese considered their country and civilization the most advanced in the world. For them, China was the "Middle Kingdom," a land located at the center of the world and surrounded by the lands of crude, uncivilized peoples they called barbarians. To protect the northern border of China, the Han emperors completed the Great Wall, and it was repaired and rebuilt down through the centuries by succeeding dynasties. The Great Wall was not a perfect barrier against invading armies, but it served well as a symbol of China's determination to keep the outside world at a distance.

41

Terra-cotta statue, Han dynasty

The ancient Chinese had many reasons to consider their civilization the greatest in the world. They knew how to make cast iron 1,500 years before Europeans. They invented papermaking, gunpowder, silk weaving, the magnetic compass, and the printing press. China's scientists made major discoveries in mathematics, astronomy, zoology, and many other sciences. China's artists painted pictures of wondrous beauty, and its writers composed superb novels and poems. Its artisans produced exquisite objects of every description for the royal family and the wealthy classes.

Many of the emperors were wise, just, and humane. Recognizing that hungry people made unruly subjects, they maintained huge granaries to feed the people in times of want. They harnessed the muscle power of the Chinese people in immense public works projects for the benefit of the populace and for the greater glory of China. With simple tools and strong backs, the ancient Chinese built the largest system of canals, flood-control dikes, and defensive walls in history. With considerable reason, the Middle Kingdom could claim the greatest cities, the most glorious palaces, and the strongest fortresses on earth. Only the Roman Empire, coming into its glory about the same time as the Han dynasty, could rival the boast.

CHINA DIVIDED

Except for one brief interruption, the Han dynasty ruled China for more than 400 years. But like dynasties before and after, the Han dynasty eventually ran out of energy. Corrupt eunuchs within the palace took control of the government, raising taxes, selling appointments for cash, and executing many honest mandarins on trumped-up charges. In A.D. 184, a great rebellion swept central China. Disgusted generals found that they could not wage effective war because the eunuchs had pilfered the military budget, sold supplies, and even taken bribes from the rebels. When the Han emperor died in A.D. 189, leaving no clear successor, the generals turned against the eunuchs. Thirty years of war followed as rival generals tried to gain control of the government. Eventually, China was divided into three kingdoms: the Wei in the north, the Wu in the south, and Shu-Han in the southwest.

The Three Kingdoms period was filled with hardship for the common people. Almost constant wars ravaged the land. Hostile tribes from north of the Great Wall conquered large areas once ruled by the Han dynasty. Dikes, canals, and roads decayed. Imperial granaries stood empty. Yet the Chinese people persisted through all the hardships, always believing that China would someday be unified again.

Wooden stature of Buddha, Song dynasty

Many Chinese sought comfort in a religion new to China: Buddhism. Like Daoism, Buddhism called on the believer to put aside worldly ambitions and desires. The first principle of Buddhism is that life is suffering—a concept that all too many Chinese found evident in their daily lives. All living beings were doomed to ride the "wheel of life" through endless cycles of birth, growth, maturity, aging, illness, and death unless they sought the enlightenment of Buddhism. Through long contemplation and rigorous denial of temptation, a person could achieve a state of perfection called Nirvana, where the self ceased to have importance and the believer could step off the endlessly repeating wheel of reincarnation.

Although occasionally suppressed by emperors jealous of the wealth amassed by the more worldly Buddhist monasteries, Buddhism survived to take its place in the assortment of beliefs accepted—often simultaneously—by the common people.

Tang court on a spring outing

THE SUI AND THE TANG

China was briefly reunified in 589 A.D. by the Sui dynasty. Like the Qin dynasty nearly eight centuries before, the Sui accomplished much in a short time. Their greatest achievement was the construction of the Grand Canal for the shipping of rice from the fertile south to the arid north. Eventually stretching some 1,050 miles (1,700 km) from Hangzhou to Beijing, the Grand Canal remains the longest canal ever built. But forced labor on the canal and the bloody cost of an unsuccessful war to conquer Korea earned the Sui the hatred of the people. Less than thirty years after coming to power, the Sui lost the mandate of Heaven.

As rebellions again swept the land, a remarkable young man named Li Shimin (A.D. 601–649) convinced his father, a provincial official, to make a bid for power. In a seven-year campaign at the head of his father's army, Li Shimin reunified China under the Tang dynasty. After his father's death, Li Shimin reigned as the Emperor T'ai Tsung from A.D. 627 to 649. Perhaps the greatest emperor in Chinese history, he used his extraordinary skills as a scholar, administrator, and soldier to weld China into the world's largest and richest empire.

The Three Pagodas of Dali,
Yunnan province, 9th and 10th centuries

After Li Shimin's death, his good-natured but lazy successor, the Emperor Gao Zong, let his wife Wu Chao (A.D. 624–705) take charge of the empire. The Empress Wu governed with great skill through her loyal and capable mandarins until forced by illness and age to give up power a few months before her death. After the brief reign of her weak son, her grandson, the Emperor Xuan Zong, became the third great Tang ruler. During his long reign (A.D. 712–756), the Tang empire reached it height. While Europe suffered through the grim decades of the early Middle Ages, a China at peace achieved spectacular growth in wealth and learning.

Near the end of Xuan Zong's reign, an ambitious general led a massive revolt against the emperor. The devastating cost of putting down the uprising tilted the Tang dynasty into a century-long decline. Power passed gradually into the hands of regional governors, who only occasionally bothered to express loyalty to the emperor. In A.D. 868, another military rebellion tipped China into chaos. The civil war lasted nearly forty years, destroying the ancient capital of Xi'an and driving the Tang from power in A.D. 907.

The cycle of Chinese history had turned again. The regional governors discarded even their casual loyalty to the central government and declared their states independent. In the north, rival generals fought for the throne of the Tang dynasty. Over the next half-century, five dynasties came and went, none of them able to control more than a third of the area once governed by the Tang.

THE RELUCTANT EMPEROR

To the vast majority of Chinese, the Five Dynasties period seemed a tremendous step backward. The people longed for a leader who would restore the unity, peace, and glory of earlier times. Their hopes were finally fulfilled in the person of Zhao Kuangyin (A.D. 927–976), a general in the army of the last of the five short-lived dynasties. One night in A.D. 960, the general was jolted awake by a group of his own soldiers entering his tent with drawn swords. He was, they announced, the new emperor whether he liked it or not.

Zhao Kuangyin's soldiers distrusted the empress who was ruling for the recently crowned infant emperor. At first unwilling, but with a growing sense of destiny, Zhao Kuangyin led his army into the capital of Kaifeng. He did not act like earlier generals who had come to overthrow an emperor and install a new dynasty. He spared the lives of the royal family and invited the government's best ministers to work for his newly declared Song dynasty. Next, the new emperor called his generals together and announced that to prevent further military uprisings, he was offering them all lavish retirements in exchange for their resignations. They all agreed.

With his base secure, Zhao Kuangyin called on the governors of the independent provinces to join him in restoring unity to China. Impressed by his wisdom and mercy, all but a few agreed. Those who chose to resist found that they could not count on their armies to fight very hard against the popular new emperor. Three years after Zhao Kuangyin's death in A.D. 976, his brother, the new emperor, brought the last of the rebellious provinces under the rule of the Song.

THE PEACEABLE SONG

The successors of Zhao Kuangyin governed the Middle Kingdom with great skill. They expanded the mandarin civil service and reduced the power of the army. Just and efficient government kept China peaceful, and the Song dynasty was never threatened by the internal revolts that had plagued earlier dynasties. The Song rulers made peace with the aggressive nomadic tribes along China's northern border in 1004, even though this meant that the Song dynasty would never hold sway over as much territory as the Tang had in its glory.

For over a century, China was at peace. The population expanded rapidly as the people prospered under benevolent taxes and laws. If crops failed or if floods washed away months of work, the government moved quickly to assist the peasants. In the cities and at court, artists, writers, and philosophers worked with renewed zest. Many Chinese in later centuries would look back on the Song period as China's golden age. But it was an age that could not last as the Middle Kingdom's riches beckoned to the restless, nomadic peoples of the north.

The Forbidden City

Chapter 4
Invaders from the North

Chinese emperors built and maintained the Great Wall to keep the fierce nomadic tribes of Mongolia and Manchuria at bay. But for all its scale and grandeur, the Great Wall could never withstand a determined invasion. In the confused period following the fall of the Tang dynasty in A.D. 907, the Khitan people of southern Mongolia occupied an area of northeastern China on either side of the Great Wall. In 1004, the Song dynasty tried to retake the territory between Beijing and the wall, but the peaceable Song never had a talent for war and soon gave up the attempt.

The Chinese and the Khitans lived in peace for more than a century. Under the influence of Chinese civilization, the Khitans abandoned their nomadic ways for a more settled life in an independent state they named Liao. With their warrior traditions forgotten, they were ill prepared to meet an invasion by another Mongolian people, the Jurchen (Kin) Tartars. The Jurchen cavalry swept through a breach in the Great Wall and smashed the Khitan army in 1124. The Song emperor of China tried to take advantage of the fighting by sending an army to occupy a piece of territory near the wall, but only succeeded in angering the Jurchen. The poorly trained and long unused Song army was no match for the hardy, warlike nomads. With the Jurchen cavalry sweeping down on the Song capital of Kaifeng, the emperor quit the throne in favor of his son.

The new emperor agreed to a truce, but unwise advisors encouraged him to attack as the Jurchen army began withdrawing. It was a disastrous blunder. The thoroughly enraged Jurchen launched an all-out invasion of China. They captured Kaifeng and then pushed south, scattering the remnants of the Song armies. A capable Song general finally stopped the Jurchen army below the Yangzi. In 1141, the Chinese and the Jurchen made peace. The Song gave up seven northern provinces—all of China north of the Huai River. For the next century, the Song governed central and southern China from the city of Hangzhou, but in this renewed era of peace, they forgot the lessons of war.

North of the Huai River, the Chinese population outnumbered their Jurchen conquerors many times over. Like the Khitans before them, the Jurchen quickly lost their nomadic identity. Within decades, they were all but absorbed into the Chinese population and culture. The Jurchen rulers had become another Chinese dynasty, hoping that the Great Wall would protect them from northern invaders. But a hurricane of devastation unlike anything the world had ever known was building in the cold, windswept grasslands of Mongolia.

Genghis Kahn

THE COMING OF THE MONGOLS

Temujin (1162?–1227), probably history's greatest conqueror and among its greatest butchers, was born into the family of a Mongol chieftain. Rivals murdered his father when Temujin was thirteen, forcing the family to flee onto the harsh Mongolian plain. They survived against long odds, and Temujin's deeds of cunning and courage won him a band of devoted followers. He reclaimed his father's chieftainship and set out to conquer all the Mongol tribes. In thirty years of almost continuous warfare, Temujin destroyed his rivals and united the Mongols into a single, incredibly warlike people. Proclaimed Genghis (Jenghiz) Khan—"universal king"—by his fellow chieftains in 1206, he prepared his Mongol hordes for a conquest that would create the largest land empire in world history.

Rapid population growth and a long warrior tradition gave Genghis Khan a large and experienced army. All Mongol males were soldiers from adolescence to old age. Conditioned by the harsh climate of their homeland, they could travel 100 miles (160 km) a day on their small, sturdy horses. At a gallop, a Mongol warrior could shoot his short, powerful bow with amazing accuracy, the arrows striking with the force to penetrate armor.

In 1210, Genghis Khan invaded the Jurchen domain in northern China. The Jurchen called on the Song dynasty for help, but the Song ignored their pleas and warnings. The Mongols raped, burned, and pillaged their way through the cradle of Chinese civilization along the Yellow River. Any city that resisted was leveled, all its inhabitants slaughtered or enslaved. Leaving generals to finish the conquest of northern China, Genghis Khan struck westward. By 1223, his hordes had swept across central Asia, Persia, and into European Russia. In 1224, Genghis Khan returned to the East. He fell on the Xixia kingdom in northwestern China, an area that had been ruled by Tibetan conquerors since the decline of the Tang dynasty more than three centuries before. The Mongols laid waste to the cities, slaughtered nearly every man, woman, and child, and left the once-prosperous Xixia kingdom a barren wilderness.

What was left of the Jurchen empire of northern China lay open to the hordes of the Great Khan. The Mongols looked on the settled, irrigated farmlands of the Chinese with disgust. One chieftain stated the common opinion: "Although we have conquered the Chinese, they are of no use to us. It would be better to exterminate them entirely, and let the grass grow so that we can have grazing land for our horses."

Fortunately for the Chinese, a remarkable man had the courage to offer a different plan. Yelu Qucai was a descendent of the Khitan royal family and a great admirer of Chinese civilization. Captured by the Mongols, he had saved his life by agreeing to become an advisor to the Khan. He convinced Genghis Khan that it made more sense to tax the captured Chinese provinces than to lay them waste. (Later Yelu Qucai played on Mongol superstitions to make them abandon their invasion of India. Perhaps no one in history saved more lives or did more to rescue great civilizations than the cunning, courageous Yelu Qucai. Yet his name is nearly forgotten while many remember the name of Genghis Khan, perhaps the greatest destroyer in history.)

Genghis Khan died in 1227. His son Ogedei (1185–1241) completed the conquest of the Jurchen empire but, following Yelu Qucai's advice, spared the country the worst of the Mongol savagery. The emperor of Song China concluded an uneasy alliance with Ogedei, and the Mongols again turned their attention to conquering the West. Ogedei's hordes defeated the Russian princes, stormed through Poland and Hungary, and were on the brink of invading Western Europe when he died in 1241. The senior Mongol generals left their armies and rushed home to cast their votes in the election of the next khan. Western Europe was saved.

After two lesser figures briefly held the khanship, Genghis Khan's grandson and Ogedei's nephew Möngke (1208–1259) became khan in 1248. Intent on equaling the conquests of his grandfather, Möngke sent his brother Hulegu to invade the Muslim Middle East while he set out to conquer the Song empire. Hulegu captured Baghdad in modern Iraq in 1258 and pushed on through Syria to within striking distance of the sacred city of Jerusalem. But once again news from the East saved one of the great cradles of civilization: Möngke had died, his conquest of Song China barely begun. Hulegu withdrew from Syria, leaving behind a portion of his army. On September 3, 1260, an Egyptian army destroyed the Mongol army at the battle of Ain Jalut near the Sea of Galilee, wrecking the fiction of Mongol invincibility and ending forever the westward push of the Mongol empire.

Kubilai Khan

Song China was not as lucky. Kubilai (1215–1294), youngest son of Ogedei, renewed the invasion of southern China. His armies pushed steadily south until, in 1279, the last Song emperor threw himself into the sea rather than surrender. For the first time since the fall of the Tang dynasty in AD 907, China was unified under a single ruler. Kubilai chose Beijing as the capital of his Yuan dynasty. Like invaders before them, the Mongols adopted many Chinese attitudes and customs.

The Yuan dynasty employed the mandarins of the fallen Song dynasty to collect the taxes and to administer China. Chinese artisans made the splendors of Kubilai's court while Chinese poets sang of its unparalleled glory. Beyond the palace walls, the Chinese people provided the muscle, brains, and energy needed to satisfy the appetites of the invaders.

END OF THE MONGOL TERROR

At its height, the Mongol empire stretched across Asia from the Pacific Ocean to the shores of the Mediterranean. But it was a fragile empire built on a foundation of military skill and raw terror, and it soon buckled under its own weight. By the 1290's, the empire had split into four separate realms. Kubilai, although in title the Great Khan, received only polite homage from the rulers of the other three khanates. After his death in 1294, his descendents fought for the throne of China, no fewer than seven emperors ruling the Yuan dynasty over the next half century.

Seething under the indignities heaped on them by the Mongols, the Chinese people rebelled in 1348. A peasant-born Buddhist monk and sometimes bandit named Zhu Yuanzhang (1328–1399) led a large rebel army in a campaign that pushed the Mongols steadily northward. In 1360, he declared himself emperor, announcing that the new Ming dynasty would rule from the great walled city of Nanjing. In 1382, Ming forces drove the last of the Mongols beyond the Great Wall. The Ming victory opened an era of great power and prosperity for China. Zhu Yuanzhang's successor, the Yongle Emperor (1360–1424), moved the capital back to Beijing, employing 200,000 workers to build a huge complex of palaces at its heart. For centuries, the Forbidden City would be off-limits to all but the most select Chinese ministers and the most prestigious foreign dignitaries.

Unlike many emperors before and most who would follow, Yongle had no fear of the outside world. He reopened the ancient caravan routes across Asia to Arabia and Europe. He sent naval expeditions to explore and trade along the coasts of Japan, Indonesia, Indochina, India, Persia, Arabia, and the east coast of Africa. His military expeditions reclaimed all the land lost to the empire since the fall of the Tang in A.D. 907.

The Yongle Emperor

But the age-old pattern of strong leaders followed by weaklings, of a dynasty in flower to a dynasty in decay, again took hold of China's fate. In the decades following Yongle's death, the Tibetans, Mongols, and Vietnamese all defeated Chinese military expeditions. Pirate fleets cruised the coastal waters, capturing trading vessels and raiding ports. Japan, unified after centuries of clan warfare, landed armies in Korea and on China's northeast coast. The Ming spent colossal sums meeting these threats. Although it was the richest country in the world, not even the prosperous Middle Kingdom could afford the cost. The Ming abandoned the rebellious frontier territories and most of their overseas trade.

THE LAST DYNASTY BEGINS

In the early 1600's, a new danger emerged as the Manchus, an aggressive Manchurian people related to the Jurchen Tartars, began challenging the power of the Ming along China's northern frontier. The overextended Ming armies retreated behind the Great Wall. Meanwhile, the cities of the south grew restless as the corrupt Ming government laid heavier and heavier taxes on the people to support the cost of defending China's borders.

As unpaid troops mutinied or deserted, an adventurer from the northwest, Li Zhicheng, led a rebel army toward Beijing. Caught between the threat of the Manchus on the north and Li Zhicheng on the West, the last Ming emperor hanged himself in the spring of 1644. A victorious Li Zhicheng entered Beijing to declare a new dynasty. He probably would have succeeded except for the personal hatred of Wu Sangui, the Ming general charged with defending the Great Wall. Wu opened the wall to the Manchus and then hunted down the fleeing Li Zhicheng while the Manchu army occupied Beijing without a fight.

For the next eighteen years, Wu Sangui fought for control of southern China against various contenders for the Ming throne. Meanwhile, the devout Shunzhi, first emperor of the Manchu Qing dynasty, ruled the north quietly and without much skill or interest. In 1661, he either died or—according to Chinese tradition— abandoned his throne for the religious life of a monastery. The new emperor was a boy of eight under the control of uncles and court eunuchs. He would eventually free himself to become one of the outstanding emperors in Chinese history, the great Kangxi (1653–1723).

Manchu guard

As Kangxi grew to manhood, China south of the Yangzi was divided into three realms governed by princes supposedly answering to the Manchu court but rarely paying it much mind. One of the princes was the formidable old soldier Wu Sangui, who neither liked nor feared the Manchus and their young emperor. In 1673, Wu Sangui threw off his allegiance to the Manchus, marching from his base in the southwest with the intention of overthrowing the dynasty and claiming the throne for his descendents. But Kangxi was no longer a boy. He won over the other princes of southern China, defeated Wu Sangui's Mongol allies, and turned back the old soldier well short of his goal. When Wu Sangui died preparing for another campaign, Kangxi launched an invasion of the southwest. Even though the other princes of southern China had sided with him against Wu Sangui, Kangxi quickly deposed them to prevent further rebellions. His army captured the rebel capital of the Wu family in 1682, exterminated the last of its members, and brought all of China under the direct rule of the Manchus. Kangzi would rule longer than any Chinese emperor in history, his reign remembered as an era of peace and prosperity.

Kangzi

Kangxi was followed by other capable emperors as China prospered for a century under the strict but efficient Qing dynasty. The dynasty's armies conquered Tibet, Mongolia, and Taiwan. Within China, the Manchus kept the people under tight control by stationing garrisons in all major cities. Like foreign dynasties before them, the Manchus depended on the Chinese mandarin class to administer the vast empire. Unlike earlier invaders who had adopted Chinese customs, the Manchus kept much of their identity. Manchu men wore their hair unbraided while native Chinese men were forced to shave the front of their scalps and wear their remaining hair in a tightly bound braid, called a *queue*, as a sign of abject submission. Manchu women did not follow the ancient Chinese custom of foot-binding: tightly bandaging the feet from infancy on to produce abnormally small feet thought beautiful by Han men. The "large" feet of Manchu women discouraged intermarriage between the Manchus and the Han Chinese and preserved the ethnic identity of the Manchus.

Although they never wholly lost their identity as foreigner invaders, the early Manchu rulers were generous patrons of China's arts, scholarship, and philosophy. Painters, writers, and calligraphers produced works of great refinement. Qing workshops turned out porcelain of a beauty unexcelled in any age. Scholars assembled monumental encyclopedias, dictionaries, and geographies to bring together more than 2,000 years of Chinese learning. Philosophers combed ancient Confucian texts in the pursuit of a perfect understanding of human character and interaction.

With the beginning of the 1800's, the energy of the dynasty began to seep away. Corruption became widespread despite the efforts of many officials of honesty and good conscience. Wealthy landlords charged exorbitant rents, forcing tens of millions of peasants into lifelong poverty. When epidemics, floods, and famines ravaged the countryside, the Qing did little to relieve the distress of the peasants. The harsh conditions led to frequent rebellions that kept much of China in turmoil for years on end.

As the Qing dynasty decayed, aggressive foreigners began eyeing China's vast riches. But these were not other Asians with at least some respect for Chinese culture but white-skinned Westerners with strange ways, fearsome weapons, and an open disdain for the Chinese. Not since the Mongol invasion six centuries before had Chinese civilization faced such a colossal challenge.

Wild Goose Pagoda, Xi'an

Chapter 5
A Collision of Cultures

Not the Great Wall or the harsh edicts of emperors could keep China isolated from the outside world. Inevitably, the "barbarians" came calling, greedy for Chinese spices, tea, porcelain, and—above all—silk. According to Chinese legend, the Empress Si Lingji, wife of the Yellow Emperor, first discovered how the cocoons of the mulberry silk moth could be woven into a luxuriant fabric. For the next 3,000 years, the craft remained a state secret, enforced by the threat of execution for anyone who whispered a word outside the imperial shops.

The first silk reached the Mediterranean world between the 6th and 4th centuries B.C. Sensationally popular with wealthy Greeks and Romans, silk became literally worth its weight in gold. To meet the demand, intrepid Arab, Turkish, and Persian traders created the Silk Route, a meandering trail stretching from Syria across some 4,000 miles (6,500 km) of plains, mountains, and deserts to the fabled Middle Kingdom. The traders traveled by camel caravan in journeys that often took years and that only the fortunate survived.

Western trader on a camel

For centuries the Silk Route provided the only link between Europe and China. A fabulous folklore about the Middle Kingdom grew up in the West, dispelled only occasionally by eyewitness reports brought back by the handful of European missionaries and traders who dared to travel the dangerous road

59

to the East. About A.D. 550, two priests bribed by the Byzantine Emperor Justinian (A.D. 483–565) smuggled silkworm eggs and the seeds of mulberry trees from China to Constantinople (modern Istanbul, Turkey) in a hollow staff. Westerners successfully cultivated the silk worm, but Chinese silk remained an exotic luxury.

During the Middle Ages, hostile Chinese emperors or wars in Central Asia closed the Silk Route for decades at a time. Yet the treasures of the Middle Kingdom continued to beckon. Late in the 13th century, the Venetian trader Marco Polo took the Silk Route to China, where he spent seventeen years in the employ Kubilai Khan. Some years after returning to Italy in 1295, Polo dictated an account of his adventures. Although *The Travels of Marco Polo* contained much inaccurate hearsay about the history of the Middle Kingdom, it remained Europe's chief source of information about China for more than two centuries.

Statue of Marco Polo in Hangzhou

In the early 1500's, Portuguese trading ships began reaching China by way of a long, dangerous voyage around the southern tip of Africa. In 1557, the reigning Ming emperor allowed the Portuguese to build a trading post at Macao, about 75 miles (120 km) south of Canton. By the mid-1600's, ships from many nations were trading at Macao, Canton, and the other ports of southern China. They brought the best the West had to offer, but found the Chinese interested in little from the barbarian lands except silver, gold, and Arabian horses.

As the number of Western traders increased over the next two centuries, the Chinese emperors became nervous about the influence of the Europeans, particularly the Christian missionaries who often accompanied the traders. In

1757, at the height of the Manchu Qing dynasty, the Emperor Qianlong confined all foreign merchants to Macao and Canton. When the Western nations objected, he dismissed their requests for open trade with the haughty reply that China already "possessed all things in prolific abundance."

THE OPIUM TRADE

The growing demand for Chinese products created a dangerous balance of trade problem for the West. The flood of silver pouring into China produced a shortage of hard currency in Europe and America. But in the late 1700's, the British found a new commodity for the China trade: the powerful narcotic drug opium. British ships from India began bringing opium into Canton in large shipments. The river of silver reversed direction, and China began to feel the economic pinch.

Chinese immigrants in an opium den in London

The medicinal uses of opium had been known in China for centuries, but the scarcity of supply had kept the price high and only a few people in the wealthy classes smoked opium for pleasure. The British importation of large amounts of opium slashed the price, and soon many Chinese in the working classes became addicts. For a few cents a person could smoke a pipe of opium and forget the backbreaking labor of the long days. But the drug left the smoker depressed, lethargic, and craving another pipe.

Recognizing the threat to the economy and the health of the people, the Chinese government tried to stamp out the opium trade. Courts ordered the execution of drug dealers and sentenced opium smokers to whippings and the public humiliation of wearing a heavy wooden collar called the *canque*. But the British traders refused to abandon their profitable business. They anchored heavily armed ships in the bay below Canton and continued selling opium to Chinese smugglers. In 1839, Chinese troops seized and destroyed a huge shipment of opium in Canton. Foreigner traders who refused to allow inspection of their goods were blockaded inside their warehouses until they cooperated. Outraged by these "attacks" on its citizens, Britain dispatched a powerful fleet to punish China. The Chinese had few warships and almost no modern weapons. The British quickly captured Shanghai, Nanjing, and a half dozen other cities, forcing the emperor to sue for peace.

Chinese war junks under fire from British warships

The British demanded harsh terms when the two sides met in Nanjing to settle the First Opium War. China paid a huge fine; opened the ports of Xiamen, Fuzhou, Ningbo, and Shanghai to foreign trade; and ceded the island of Hong Kong to Britain. As the British began building Hong Kong into one of the world's richest trading centers, other Western powers rushed to force treaties on the defeated dynasty. The Chinese gave in to demands for "extraterritoriality," the right of the Western powers to establish self-governing enclaves in the newly opened treaty ports. Western administrators, judges, and imported troops and police would enforce Western laws and customs within these "concession areas." In addition, any Westerner accused of breaking the law anywhere in China would be tried not in a local Chinese court but in a Western court in a concession area. Chinese gangs moved their headquarters into the concession areas, where they could organize their far-flung criminal activities beyond the reach of Chinese law. Western authorities looked the other way or openly collaborated with the gangsters.

BLOODY REBELLIONS

The humiliation of the Qing dynasty at the hands of the Westerners set the Chinese masses seething. The Manchu emperors had never been popular, and many Chinese felt that the dynasty had lost the mandate of Heaven. Rebellions broke out across China. For years, rebels—some of them no more than common bandits—controlled large sections of rural China.

In the late 1840's, a strange and magnetic man took advantage of the unrest to launch the largest rebellion in Chinese history. Hong Xiuquan (1813–1864) was a member of the Hakka minority of southern China. His family had made sacrifices to prepare him for the government examinations that would give him a secure place in the civil service. But Hong repeatedly failed the examinations. Despondent, he fell ill. In a fever, he had a vision of a golden-haired man who called him younger brother. Some years later, while working as a village schoolteacher, Hong read a Christian missionary pamphlet and thought he recognized the golden-haired man as Jesus Christ.

Hong became a passionate convert to Christianity, spreading the religion he only sketchily understood among the downtrodden peasants and miners of Guangxi province. Hong's Society of God Worshippers grew with amazing speed. The God Worshippers tore down "pagan" temples, denounced the rigid Confucian principles that governed Chinese society, and drilled in preparation for a war to drive the hated Manchus back into the "wilderness" beyond the Great Wall. In the rugged Thistle Mountain region of eastern Guangxi, Hong set up a social organization unlike anything China had ever seen. Men and women were segregated: living, working, and drilling in separate organizations. Alcohol and opium were forbidden. Converts gave all their money and valuables to the common treasury. Land was held in common with all working according to their abilities and receiving according to their needs. In this respect particularly, Hong's followers practiced a socialist principle that would later become the central ideal of communism in China and the Soviet Union.

Hong Xiuquan

The growing number and militancy of Hong's followers finally attracted the attention of the lethargic government. In December 1850, a Qing army advanced on Hong's mountain stronghold, only to be soundly defeated by the God Worshippers. In the flush of victory, Hong declared himself Taiping Tianguo—"the Emperor of Great Peace from the Heavenly Kingdom"—a title that gave his followers their common name, the Taiping. The Taiping army marched out of the mountains to overthrow the Qing dynasty. After gaining experience in some early failures, the rebels pushed north with a series of extraordinary victories. As city after city fell, tens of thousands of converts flocked to Hong's banner. In March 1854, Hong captured the great city of Nanjing. His followers butchered 40,000 Manchu men, women, and children in a terrible revenge on the "devils" from north of the Great Wall.

If Hong had continued his march north toward Beijing, he probably would have driven the Qing from power. But he let the chance slip away. Instead, he lived in luxury among his concubines while searching the Bible for references to his "mission." Several of his most able lieutenants engaged in a power struggle and were either assassinated or fled Nanjing. Many Chinese, who had earlier viewed the Taiping rebels as heroic freedom fighters, were horrified by their attacks on traditional religious symbols and

Confucian standards. Many Westerners, particularly in the missionary community, at first sympathized with the Taiping cause, but they became disenchanted when they learned of the more bizarre aspects of Hong's faith and Taiping social organization. Western business interests preferred to deal with the weak Qing dynasty rather than a possible Taiping dynasty that would carry out Hong's promise to destroy the opium trade and to end extraterritorial rights in the treaty ports.

As dedicated mandarin generals rallied the Qing armies, the Western powers dispatched gunboats and military advisors to help in the fight against the Taiping. An American adventurer, Frederick Townsend Ward, drilled a Chinese army in the use of modern firearms and Western tactics. After Ward's death, a British artillery officer, Charles "Chinese" Gordon (1833–1885), led the "Ever Victorious Army" in a campaign that destroyed the Taiping's reputation for invincibility. Shortly after Hong's death in the summer of 1864, government armies stormed Nanjing. An awed general reported to the emperor: "Not one of the 100,000 rebels...surrendered...but in many cases gathered together and burned themselves and passed away without repentance. Such a formidable band of rebels has been rarely known from ancient times to the present."

Charles Gordon

A TOTTERING DYNASTY

The Taiping rebellion cost an estimated 20 million lives and destroyed all but the last shreds of the Qing dynasty's mandate to rule. Even while Chinese armies were using Western aid to fight the Taiping, the Western powers were dispatching ships and soldiers to force new treaties on the dynasty. In the Second Opium War or Arrow War (1856–1860), British troops occupied Beijing, burning the glorious Imperial Palace in a wanton act of vandalism. China's defeat by Britain and France led to the opening of eleven more treaty ports and the ceding of coastal areas surrounding Hong Kong's harbor to the British.

The dynasty tottered, too corrupt and weak to govern effectively. The vast majority of Chinese lived in brutal poverty. With 90% of the land owned by rich landlords, the peasants worked at starvation wages. Some Christian missionaries tried to help the poor, but most Westerners were too intent on making money to pay much attention to the suffering of the Chinese people.

Cixi

In 1861, the Empress Dowager Cixi (1835–1908) became China's ruler as regent for her son, the child-emperor Tongzhi. After his death in 1875, she continued as regent for the even younger Emperor Guangxu (1871–1908).

Intelligent, but unfamiliar with the ways of the wider world and under the influence of dishonest eunuchs, she attempted to rule China like an empress of old. She spent extravagantly, once using funds intended for the modernization of the Chinese navy on an immense marble boat at the Summer Palace.

THE OVERSEAS CHINESE

Despite the terrible death toll brought by frequent famines and revolts, China's population continued to expand. By the 1870's, 400 million Chinese were stretching the nation's resources to the limit. Millions fled the poverty and disorder in the countryside only to find life equally hard in the teeming, filthy slums of China's cities. The government promoted a pioneer movement into China's sparsely settled west, but harsh natural conditions and the hostility of non-Chinese tribes limited internal expansion.

Chinese immigrants aboard SS *Alaska*

Millions of coastal Chinese took the difficult step of leaving their homeland. Boatloads of emigrants sailed from the ports of China. Many Chinese settled in the countries of Southeast Asia, where they took up their traditional vocations of farming, fishing, and shopkeeping. Some later became wealthy in business, mining, rubber planting, and shipping.

Foreign contractors signed up armies of Chinese laborers for the even longer trip across the Pacific to the Americas. The passage was brutal, the laborers packed so tightly in the holds of the ships that they could hardly lie down. In Hawaii, South America, and the Caribbean islands, they were put to work in mines or on sugar plantations. Cheated of their pay, forced to work inhuman hours, and often whipped and chained, they became little more than slaves.

Large numbers of Chinese immigrants began to reach the West Coast of the United States near the end of the California gold rush of 1848–1849. Too late to make fortunes in the gold fields, they worked abandoned claims and then began to drift into other occupations as shopkeepers, laundry operators, and vegetable gardeners. Thousands signed on to build the first transcontinental railroads. By the 1880's, nearly every city in North America had its Chinese community.

Chinese immigrants work a California gold claim.

Chinese immigrants faced widespread hostility in a land where their customs, language, dress, and skin color differed greatly from the European-American majority. Chinese workers accepted low wages and long hours, angering American workers often in competition for the same jobs. Many Chinese immigrants expressed an ambition to return home once they had saved enough money to live comfortably in China—an attitude that deeply offended many Americans. Inflamed by racist speakers and hate-filled newspapers, American workers attacked Chinese immigrants in a series of vicious riots.

In 1882, the United States Congress passed the Chinese Exclusion Act, imposing a ban on the immigration of Chinese laborers, requiring all resident

Chinese to carry registration certificates, and barring all Chinese from seeking American citizenship. Although some of the clauses were not enforced after the turn of the century, the Exclusion Act was not entirely abolished until 1946.

Li Hongzhang

CALLS FOR REFORM

Even the emigration of millions could not ease the pressures building in China. A few brave scholars had been urging reform on the Qing dynasty for a century and more, only to be ignored, banished, or executed. With the 20th century rapidly approaching, a broader group of scholars called on the government to take radical action before it was too late. Students educated abroad and overseas Chinese added their voices to the calls for reform. They had seen the industrial might of the West, tasted firsthand the freedoms of democracy, and come to understand that China could not prosper without putting aside some of its ancient ways.

A powerful and upright Qing minister, Li Hongzhang (1823–1901), promoted a "self-strengthening" movement to import Western technology and methods while preserving the best in traditional Chinese culture. He developed programs to send bright Chinese students to universities in Europe, the United States, and Japan; encouraged the building of railroads and modern factories; and engineered the construction of a small modern navy. Yet all of Li Hongzhang's diplomatic skill could not save China from the imperial designs of the Western powers. In the early 1880's, the French occupied northern Vietnam, ignoring Chinese claims to special privileges in the area. When negotiations broke down in 1884, the French fleet in the southern Chinese port of Fuzhou opened fire, destroying half of China's new "self-strengthening" fleet in an hour.

THE SINO-JAPANESE WAR

In 1894, the Qing received yet another brutal lesson in China's near helplessness against modern technology. Recently modernized Japan was the teacher. Japan had closed its ports to foreign traders in the 1630's, refusing to deal with the outside world for more than two centuries. But in 1853, an American naval squadron under Commodore Matthew Perry (1794–1858) sailed into Tokyo Bay to deliver a letter from the president of the United States suggesting a commercial treaty. The Japanese leaders were stunned by the size and firepower of the American warships. They quickly recognized what the Chinese emperors had not: to compete with the industrialized West, they would have to modernize. In an amazing transformation, the Japanese changed their country from a medieval society into a modern state in a single generation. Confident and aggressive, Japan set out to dominate Asia.

Korea became Japan's first target. For centuries, Korean kings had paid homage to Chinese emperors, accepting—often unwillingly— China's role as Korea's protector. When a rebellion broke out in the Korean capital of Seoul in the summer of 1894, China dispatched troops to protect the Korean royal family. But Japan, uninvited and unwanted, moved faster. Japanese armed forces occupied Seoul and ambushed unsuspecting Chinese troops en route to Korea. China tried to fight, but its forces were no match for the well-armed and well-trained Japanese. By the spring of 1895, China's fleet lay on the ocean bottom and its best troops were in headlong retreat toward Beijing. Forced to accept another humiliating peace treaty, China surrendered all influence over Korea, opened four more ports to foreign trade, paid a huge fine, and turned over the island province of Taiwan to Japan.

As China lay helpless, the great powers began slicing it into "spheres of influence," where they, not the Chinese government, ruled in all but name. Britain took the fertile Yangzi Valley. Russia controlled Manchuria and Mongolia. Germany, France, and Japan seized large coastal areas. Coming too late to the party, the United States in 1899 called for an "open door" policy that would preserve "the territorial and administrative integrity" of China while granting all nations equal trading rights in the world's most populous nation. The other great powers refused to agree, but the Open Door became the basis for America's foreign policy toward China and the eventual source of explosive friction with Japan.

Chinese battleship *Zhenyuan*

THE HUNDRED DAYS REFORM

In the bitter aftermath of China's defeat by Japan, the calls for reform became a din. The reformers gained the ear of the young emperor Guangxu, urging him to free himself from the influence of his aging and conservative aunt, the Empress Dowager Cixi. While Cixi was absent from the capital in the summer of 1898, Guangxu began a startling series of reforms. For the next hundred days, a stream of decrees came from the palace. Henceforth, schools would teach both Chinese and Western subjects. The old civil service exams, based on the Confucian classics, would undergo radical updating. A restructured civil service would attract and promote people equipped with modern skills. The military would get the funds needed to become an effective fighting force. There would be a complete overhaul of the court system and the nation's often cruel and arbitrary laws. Police and prosecutors would root out corruption from the smallest village to the palace itself.

The reforms represented a direct assault on the power and privilege of Cixi's ruling elite. The enraged empress dowager returned to Beijing in September. Backed by powerful allies, she ordered Guangxu arrested and imprisoned on an island in the lake at the Summer Palace, executed many of his leading advisors, and withdrew nearly all the reform decrees. Within days, all the promise of the reform movement lay in ruin. The dynasty returned to its corrupt and backward ways.

Stereoptic image of Boxers on the march

THE BOXER REBELLION

As the new century opened, more Chinese focused their anger on the "foreign devils" busily carving up China "like a huge melon." Tens of thousands of Chinese joined the violently anti-foreign Society of Righteous and Harmonious Fists. The Boxers, as they were called by Westerners, had no central leadership and no consistent program except to drive the "foreign devils" from China as a first step in restoring the Middle Kingdom to its ancient glory. In 1900, Boxer violence swept across northern China. The Boxers executed hundreds of missionaries and Western traders and thousands of their Chinese converts and employees. As a horde of Boxers streamed into Beijing, the Qing government abandoned its effort to put down the rebellion and began calling the rebels a loyal militia. The Boxers laid siege to Beijing's legation (foreign embassy) quarter for eight weeks, but they were too disorganized to overcome the small number of Western troops and armed civilians inside.

On August 14, 1900, some 20,000 Western troops marched into Beijing. The Boxers and the royal family fled the city. The Western powers took a terrible revenge. Western troops hunted down the Boxers—sometimes with the aid of missionaries—executing without trial even those only suspected of being sympathetic to the movement. Troops and civilians looted everything they could find of value and bragged about it in the newspapers. The Qing government was fined a crushing $333 million—nearly two times its annual budget—for its part in the uprising.

The tragic emperor Guangxu

REFORM COMES TOO LATE

Allowed to keep her throne, Cixi reluctantly instituted some of the reforms that Guangxu had attempted. Both the emperor and Cixi died in the same month in 1908—she of old age, he allegedly of poison administered at her order. One of Cixi's last acts was to promise the Chinese people a constitutional monarchy in which the emperor would be a figurehead and the real power would rest with the people. But it was too late. Not even massive reform could save the system that had ruled China since the Qin dynasty over 2000 years before.

Monument outside Mao's Mausoleum

Chapter 6
Decades of Turmoil

In the first years of the 20th century, thousands of Chinese joined underground revolutionary organizations. Based in China's teeming cities, the revolutionary groups included students, professionals, soldiers, shopkeepers, industrial workers, and representatives of nearly every walk of life. All shared the common goal of destroying the doddering Qing dynasty and restoring China's independence from foreign domination. Some groups concentrated on spreading their vision of a better society through speeches and radical newspapers. Others went beyond words as they tried to foment revolution through assassination and sabotage.

The child emperor Puyi

The fall of the last dynasty came with remarkable speed and little bloodshed by the standards of Chinese history. On October 9, 1911, an explosion ripped through a secret bomb factory in the city of Hankou in east-central China. Qing police investigating the accident found documents listing the names of soldiers who had enrolled in the revolutionary underground. Threatened with exposure and probable execution, soldiers in nearby Wuchang mutinied early the next morning. The mutiny spread rapidly as garrisons in a dozen other cities announced that they would no longer take orders from the Qing government. Senior army officers refused to put down the mutiny, calling instead for massive reforms, including the formation of a national parliament and the election of a premier to govern the country.

In a desperate attempt to save the dynasty, the mother of the child-emperor Puyi (1905–1967), the son of the unfortunate Guangxu, agreed to surrender most of the dynasty's power to a premier: the reformist provincial governor Yuan Shikai (1859–1916). However, provincial assemblies meeting in Nanjing refused to accept a constitutional monarchy, declaring China a republic and electing as president Dr. Sun Yat-sen (1866–1925).

Dr. Sun Yat-sen

Dr. Sun was already a world-renowned figure. Educated in mission schools in Hawaii and a Western medical school in Hong Kong, he became a revolutionary activist in his twenties. In 1895, after a failed plot to overthrow the dynasty, he fled China, eventually settling in London. Qing agents tried to kidnap him, but he made a daring escape and recounted his dramatic story in the Western newspapers. The resulting fame allowed him to travel widely, seeking support from overseas Chinese and sympathetic Westerners for a republican revolution in China. He developed a program of three principles for a new China: nationalism (the people should strive to build a strong China capable of managing its own affairs); democracy (government by the people through elected representatives); and "the people's livelihood" (the wealth of China should be managed for the good of all).

Dr. Sun accepted the presidency of the republic declared by the provincial assemblies. But to avoid civil war between his government in Nanjing and Yuan Shikai's in Beijing, he offered to resign in favor of Yuan if the Qing dynasty gave up its remaining power. Under pressure from Yuan and senior army officers, the royal family agreed to step down in exchange for an annual income and continued residence in Beijing's Forbidden City. On February 12, 1912, the little boy Puyi—the last emperor of China—abdicated and became a private, although very wealthy, citizen. Dr. Sun resigned, and Yuan Shikai became president.

THE REVOLUTION BETRAYED

China held its first national election in January 1913. Dr. Sun's Guomindang party (usually referred to by Westerners as the Nationalist party) won a large majority of seats in the new parliament. Unfortunately for China, President Yuan Shikai had little real sympathy for democracy. When Guomindang delegates harshly criticized his handling of the nation's finances, he fired all pro-Guomindang military governors and sent his troops to destroy Guomindang strongholds. With the Guomindang driven underground, Dr. Sun fled to Japan. The ambitious Yuan tried to found a new dynasty, but he lacked the money and military power to impose his will on a China sick of emperors.

In 1914, World War I tore Europe apart. While the Europeans concentrated on killing each other in incredible numbers and the United States tried to avoid foreign involvements, Japan moved swiftly to fill the power void in China. Japan seized Germany's sphere of influence on China's northern coast and delivered a long list of demands to Yuan Shikai. The Japanese wanted extraordinary privileges in China, including the right to oversee the workings of the Chinese government and police force. Although

Yuan had courted the support of the Japanese in founding his new dynasty, they were demanding too much in return. He sought Western support in refusing Japan's Twenty-one Demands, but the European powers were too busy and the United States put no teeth behind its objection. Threatened by Japan's modern army and navy, Yuan gave in to most of the demands.

Yuan Shikai died in 1916, his dreams of a new dynasty in tatters. The central government in Beijing became a shaky coalition of military leaders. Some were educated and patriotic, others mere bandits in uniform. Each warlord ruled his own region, often fighting his neighbors. As always in times of political division, the common people suffered greatly. Dr. Sun Yat-sen returned to China to begin the long task of rebuilding his Guomindang movement. Meanwhile, the war in Europe raged, chewing up an entire generation of young men. On the urging of Britain, France, Japan, and particularly President Woodrow Wilson (1856–1924) of the United States, the Beijing government declared war on Germany. Some 100,000 Chinese laborers traveled halfway around the globe to unload ships, build barracks, and dig trenches for the Allies.

When Germany surrendered in 1918, China expected recognition of its contribution to Allied victory. But the Treaty of Versailles in 1919 gave the German concession area in Shandong province to Japan rather than returning it to the control of the Beijing government. The Chinese were appalled. On May 4, 1919, thousands of Chinese students gathered in Tiananmen Square at the center of Beijing to denounce the treaty and several cabinet ministers suspected of conspiring with the Japanese. Marching on the Japanese embassy, the students collided with club-swinging police who killed one student and left scores injured. News of the clash sparked sympathy strikes and demonstrations across China. The protests gave birth to the May 4th Movement, an attempt to redefine Chinese culture to fit the modern world and to unite the people against the evils of warlordism, the landlord system, and foreign imperialism.

As the forces of revolution gathered again, a great drought devastated central China. Forced to pay outrageous rents, the peasant farmers had little cash or food in reserve. Between 1919 and 1921, 500,000 people died of starvation and some 20 million—40% of the area's estimated population—were left destitute. Conditions in many of China's crowded cities were barely better. Once again, the cry went up across China for a strong, united, and just central government that could respond to the people's needs.

Karl Marx

THE DREAM OF COMMUNISM

Bitterly disappointed with the hypocrisy of the Treaty of Versailles, some young Chinese rejected the Western democratic model. For them, the radical philosophy of communism seemed a shining hope for China.

The underlying idea of communism is very old: private property is evil. Throughout history, many thinkers concluded that greed for money and possessions always created a society of "haves and have-nots." They theorized that a better society could be built if property were held in common. All members of society would labor for the common good, receiving the necessities of life according to their needs. In the history of both East and West, there were numerous attempts to put communism into practice. Religious orders, utopian societies, and revolutionary groups—among them the Taiping—tried again and again. Bickering within destroyed most of the experiments while the more threatening were suppressed, often with great bloodshed, by hostile churches or governments.

The German philosopher Karl Marx (1818–1883) laid out the framework of modern "scientific" communism. Marx stated that history could be explained as a conflict between the upper classes who owned the "means of production" and the working classes who provided the labor but received only a tiny percentage of the profits in wages. Marx believed that the world's workers (the proletariat) would eventually rise up to seize the means of

79

production. During a period of state socialism directed by a "dictatorship of the proletariat," a harmonious, classless society would evolve to make government unnecessary, thus allowing the state to "wither away."

Marx's theories attracted a small but highly dedicated following in Europe and America. In 1903, the revolutionary V. I. Lenin (1870–1924) helped found a Russian communist party, the Bolsheviks, to overthrow the Russian emperors, the czars. The Bolsheviks had little success until heavy losses in World War I brought Russia near to collapse. In February 1917, hungry, war-weary workers in the Russian capital of St. Petersburg rebelled against the czarist government. Czar Nicholas II abdicated as the revolt spread to the armed forces, and Russia's legislature, the *Duma*, elected a government of moderate reformers. But the new government enjoyed little popular support and made the gigantic mistake of continuing the war against Germany.

Lenin

THE BOLSHEVIK REVOLUTION

Lenin, who had returned to St. Petersburg from exile in Switzerland, plotted the overthrow of the faltering reform government. In November 1917, the Bolsheviks staged a successful coup to take over the government. Russia's new leaders immediately pulled Russia out of the war and announced the formation of a communist state. Russia and the subject nations that had been part of the czarist empire became the Union of Soviet Socialist Republics (USSR).

The USSR won many Chinese friends in July 1919 when it announced that it would return the Russian sphere of influence in Mongolia and northern Manchuria to Chinese control. Chinese radicals sought Soviet help in forming a communist party in China. As the main sponsor of the international communist organization, the Comintern, the Soviets were more than willing to help. Comintern agents traveled to China, where they conducted classes in Marxist-Leninist theory and the practical methods of revolutionary organization.

The Comintern agents selected able and dedicated Chinese students for advanced training in the USSR, France, and Japan. Among those who traveled to Paris in 1920 was an exceptionally gifted young man named Zhou Enlai. The son of a prominent mandarin family, Zhou had received an excellent education, spoke several languages, and—even at the age of twenty-one—had the courtly manners of a diplomat. In a different century, he might have followed the traditional mandarin path through the examination system to a position of power in the imperial government. But the times made him a radical, and he had already served time in jail for helping organize the May 4th demonstrations.

Zhou's name would be linked in the decades to come with that of another young revolutionary: Mao Zedong. Mao came from a very different background. The son of a moderately well off farming family in Hunan province, Mao had received a classical education as a child. While serving briefly as a soldier in the 1911 revolution against the Qing dynasty, he was deeply moved by the poverty and suffering he saw in rural China. He rejected life on the family farm and a marriage arranged by his parents in favor of a life of political activism. He moved to the city of Changsha, where he read widely in the political philosophy of East and West. In 1917, he began publishing a series of articles on the importance of physical exercise, equality for women, and the solidarity of the people in the revolutionary struggle against warlordism, imperialism, and the class system.

By 1921, Mao had become a leading organizer of radical activity in Hunan province. That July he traveled to Shanghai to meet with a handful of like-minded radicals. Meeting in secret, they formed the Chinese Communist Party (CCP). Zhou Enlai was still in France, but he would join the CCP soon after his return to China. Other Communists with longer experience in revolutionary activity took the leading roles in the early years, but Mao and Zhou would eventually become the principal shapers of Chinese communism.

THE GUOMINDANG AND THE CCP

Dr. Sun Yat-sen's Guomindang party and the CCP shared the common goals of national reunification and an end to foreign imperialism. However, Dr. Sun opposed other aspects of communism, particularly the rigid state socialism of the Soviet model that did away with private enterprise and threatened personal initiative. At first Dr. Sun refused to allow Communists to join the Guomindang. But in 1922 Lenin began loosening the grip of the state over economic activity in the USSR. Lenin's New Economic Policy (NEP) persuaded Dr. Sun that he might be able to work with the Communists after all. He accepted Soviet aid and promised to admit individual Communists to the Guomindang if the CCP gave up its faith in the Soviet model and disbanded its formal structure.

Deeply concerned with the growing influence of Japan in the Far East, Soviet advisors pressured the Chinese Communists into a public acceptance of Dr. Sun's conditions. But rather than disbanding, the CCP became an underground organization, recruiting converts and preparing for the time when Guomindang victory would unify the nation and end the interference of foreign powers in China's affairs. Then the CCP could emerge to make its bid for supreme power.

Chiang Kai-shek and Dr. Sun

THE NATIONALIST REVOLUTION

In February 1923, Dr. Sun established a Nationalist government in Canton. The Soviet Union poured money into the creation of a well-armed and well-trained Nationalist army. A Soviet advisor, Mikhail Borodin (1884–1951), helped the Nationalists establish a military academy on Whampoa Island downriver from Canton. Borodin skillfully balanced Guomindang and CCP influence at the academy. The first commandant was Chiang Kai-shek (1887–1975), a military advisor to Dr. Sun, while the political director was an ardent CCP member, the charming and sophisticated Zhou Enlai. Within a year, the academy produced the first crop of tough young officers to lead the Nationalist armies to victory.

Dr. Sun died on March 12, 1925, and Chiang Kai-shek became the dominant member of the Nationalist leadership. His army had already won its first victories against the southern warlords, and Chiang judged that conditions would soon be right for an all-out campaign to unify China. The country seethed with rage against the corruption of warlords and the outrages of foreigners. Mao Zedong, Zhou Enlai, and hundreds of other Communist organizers were at work fomenting discontent among rural peasants and city workers. The Communist organizers set up people's governments, called soviets.

The soviets attacked social problems such as crime, drug addiction, prostitution, and the selling of children in hard times. In the countryside, the peasant soviets confiscated land from the rich and redistributed it among poor farmers. In the cities, worker soviets organized strikes and demonstrations against Chinese and foreign companies guilty of exploiting their Chinese workers. Local authorities, both Chinese and Western, struck back hard. In Canton and Shanghai, British troops fired on demonstrators, killing dozens.

In July 1926, Chiang set his military campaign in motion. Three Nationalist armies pushed steadily through southern China toward the Yangzi. Ahead of the armies, Communist agents organized local uprisings. Westerners fled in droves, often under the protective fire of Western warships. Some warlords joined Chiang's advancing armies, others were crushed in heavy fighting. By early 1927, the Nationalist armies had captured all of southeastern China and were advancing on China's largest city, the great port of Shanghai.

While the army won victory after victory, there was bitter infighting between the conservative Chiang and more radical Guomindang and Communist leaders. Chiang made Nanchang his military base while the radicals set up a national government in Wuhan. The Communists took a leading role in the Wuhan government, pushing for drastic economic and political reforms in the territory won by the Nationalist armies. The activities of the Communists threatened Chiang's dominance of the Nationalist cause and put at risk the welfare of many of his influential and wealthy supporters. Chiang began plotting the destruction of the Communists and the Guomindang radicals.

Still youthful in 1938, Zhou Enlai, his wife Deng Yingchao, and the American journalist Edgar Snow

In March 1927, as Chiang's troops surrounded Shanghai, Zhou Enlai led an uprising that established a Communist government in the city. Chiang was furious; the Communists were out of control. He met secretly with leaders of the city's underworld Green Gang, headquartered in the French concession area. On April 12, with the support of the city's Western authorities, the Green Gang attacked the Communists. Chiang's troops joined in the slaughter. Only a small percentage of the Communists, including Zhou, managed to escape into the countryside.

Mao (at right) and his family in 1919

Chiang established a government in Nanjing and demanded that the Wuhan government disband. In the countryside, his troops killed thousands of peasants who had joined the Communist soviets. Communist revolts in Nanchang and Canton were suppressed with incredible brutality. The surviving Communists went into hiding, their Comintern advisors fled China, and the Wuhan government collapsed. His position as undisputed leader of the government secured, Chiang began planning the conquest of China north of the Yangtze.

THE JIGSAW NORTH

Since the death of Yuan Shikai in 1916, northern China had been divided among warlords. Chiang expected most of them to cooperate with the Nationalists once his armies crossed the Yangtze. However, the wily Manchurian warlord Zhang Zuolin (1875–1928), who had occupied Beijing in late 1924, promised to be a major obstacle in the way of a Nationalist victory. Chiang's second great concern was a Japanese army protecting the foreign concession areas in the port of Tianjin and the Yellow River city of Jinan. A third threat lay farther north in the form of the Japanese Kwantung army protecting Japan's sphere of influence in Manchuria, China's vast northeastern province.

If anything, Zhang Zuolin faced an even more difficult situation. With the Communists on the run, Chiang had the temporary luxury of a secure home base. Zhang Zuolin, however, had to worry about the restless Kwantung army. Zhang Zuolin hated the Japanese, but he lacked the military force to drive the Kwantung army out of Manchuria. The officers of the Kwantung army, who despised Zhang Zuolin, wanted to attack the warlord and take control of all of Manchuria. But Japan's civilian government opposed any drastic action that might draw heavy criticism from the Western powers and cause trouble with the Soviet Union's forces along Manchuria's northern border.

The confused situation in Manchuria had been decades in the making. Members of Japan's ancient and powerful military class had coveted the resources of China since Japan's rapid modernization in the late 19th century. In the Sino-Japanese War of 1894–95, Japan's armed forces had taken control of Korea, long a dependency of China. A decade later, Japan had dealt the Russians a stunning defeat in the Russo-Japanese War to establish a sphere of influence in the southern half of Manchuria. Resource-poor Japan poured huge sums into the development of mines, factories, and railroads in Manchuria. To protect these investments, the Japanese government established the Kwantung army of tough Mongolian mercenaries and well-trained Japanese soldiers. Most of the Kwantung army's Japanese officers were aggressive militarists who dreamed of a time when the Japanese army would sweep south in a great campaign to bring all of China—and eventually all of eastern Asia—under the domination of Japan.

Militarists controlled the Japanese government through World War I. With the Western powers distracted by the war in Europe, Japan brought heavy diplomatic and military pressure to bear on China with the Twenty-one Demands. Following World War I, however, the Western powers again took an interest in China, and Japan had to assume a less aggressive stance. Gradually, liberal democratic parties opposed to the militarists gained the upper hand in Japan's government, but the Kwantung army remained a stronghold of militarist sentiment. As Chiang began his march north in early 1928, officers in the Kwantung army devised a plot that they hoped would free them of both Zhang Zuolin and the pesky liberals at home.

THE NATIONALIST OFFENSIVE

Late in the winter of 1928, Chiang crossed the Yangtze and marched on Beijing. Several of the remaining warlords came over to Chiang's side, and most of the foreign powers extended grudging recognition to the Nationalist government. As the army neared the Yellow River, Chiang asked the Japanese to withdraw their troops from the river city of Jinan. At first it appeared that they would, but on May 3 a skirmish between the two armies turned into a pitched battle. Driven back from the city, Chiang rerouted his march and pushed on toward Beijing.

With the Nationalist armies descending on Beijing, Zhang Zuolin looked for an escape. The Japanese assured him that they would keep the Nationalists from advancing beyond the Great Wall if he would abandon Beijing and return to Manchuria. Zhang Zuolin agreed and loaded his staff aboard a train bound for the Manchurian capital of Mukden. A few miles short of Mukden, bombs exploded under the train, killing the warlord and many in his party.

Plotters in the Kwantung army had placed the bombs. They expected that the death of Zhang Zuolin would create a crisis in the Japanese government. Panicked by the threat to Japan's vital sphere of influence in southern Manchuria by the Nationalists to the south and the Soviets to the north, the government's civilian ministers would place the armed services on a war footing. The mobilization of the armed services would put militarists in position to sweep the civilian ministers aside and to order the occupation of all of Manchuria. If Chiang advanced north of the Great Wall, so much the better; the Japanese army would crush him and seize all of northern China.

Scene of the bombing of Zhang Zoulin's train

The dreams of the Kwantung officers failed to materialize. Resolute liberals in the Japanese government refused to be stampeded into mobilization, and Chiang skillfully ducked confrontation. With the support of both the Nationalist and Japanese governments, Zhang Zuolin's son, Zhang Xueliang (1898–2001) took command of his father's army. The "Young Marshal," as Zhang Xeuliang became known, proved a surprisingly competent successor to his father, despite a reputation as a playboy and a drug addict. He assured the Japanese government of Japan's continued privileges in Manchuria while at the same time pledging loyalty to Chiang and accepting a seat in the Nationalist State Council. A brooding Kwantung army, left with no one to fight, went back to protecting Japanese-owned railroads and mines. The Young Marshal raised the Nationalist flag over Mukden. For the first time since the fall of the Qing dynasty, China was united.

Much of the outside world applauded the Nationalist victory, but the new government brought little relief to the majority of China's common people, who continued to live a life of terrible rural poverty. Chiang ruled as a dictator over an almost unbelievably corrupt government. New warlords controlled half the country, sometimes collecting taxes fifty years in advance. Landlords bought up more land, making the life of the peasants even harder. Between 1928 and 1930, five million people starved to death and 400,000 peasants sold themselves or their children into servitude.

THE COMMUNISTS REBUILD

Badly wounded in Chiang's 1927 purge, the Communist Party rebuilt in the mountains of Jiangxi province in southeastern China. Many of its early leaders were dead, and Mao Zedong and Zhou Enlai rose to senior positions in the reconstructed Party.

Mao rethought the CCP's plans for revolution. In Russia, Lenin and his followers had organized industrial workers and managed to grab power with only a tiny minority of the country's population. But Chiang's army had crushed the worker soviets in China's cities with little difficulty. For a Communist revolution to succeed in China, Mao concluded, the CCP would have to mobilize the great mass of peasants. After a long and heated debate, the leadership agreed. The CCP turned its attention to strengthening the rural soviets that had survived Chiang's purge. The CCP issued strict rules for its political organizers and the soldiers of its Red Army. There would be no looting, no raping, no abuse of the peasants. Troops would pay for what they ate. All would treat the peasants with respect.

Alarmed at the CCP's renewed activity, Chiang pushed his ongoing campaign against the Communists. In the immensity of rural China, it was a difficult task, but Chiang's troops made steady progress in snuffing out the rural soviets.

THE JAPANESE MILITARISTS STRIKE

Japanese militarists had not given up their ambitions after the failed plot in Manchuria in 1928. On September 18, 1931, Kwantung agents set off bombs along the railway line outside the Manchurian capital of Mukden. They blamed the blasts on some of Zhang Xueliang's troops in the area and used the lie as an excuse to seize Mukden. Crack Japanese divisions poured in from nearby Korea, inflicting heavy losses on the Young Marshal's unprepared army. In Japan, senior army and navy officers demanded the government's full support. Cowed by the militarists, the civilian ministers accepted a conflict that they had tried to prevent.

Japanese troops on the march

Chiang Kai-shek was desperate to avoid war with Japan. He ordered Zhang Xueliang to retreat south of the Great Wall. By year's end, the Japanese occupied all of Manchuria. They installed Puyi, the last Chinese emperor and now a young man in his twenties, as the puppet ruler of a new state they named Manchukuo.

The Western powers objected to Japan's aggression but did nothing meaningful to force a Japanese withdrawal. Several factors contributed to the West's declining interest in China. The West's industrialized nations had severe problems at home as the world's economy staggered through the Great Depression, the decade of hard times that had begun in 1929. The European nations had never recovered from World War I and no longer had the power or the will to oppose Japanese expansion. The United States had adopted a policy of "isolationism," avoiding foreign involvement wherever possible. America's refusal to join the League of Nations, the international peacekeeping organization established after World War I, left the League powerless to intervene in China.

After a few feeble protests, the West turned to other problems, leaving the Japanese militarists to make plans for conquering a gigantic empire that they politely called the "Greater East Asian Co-Prosperity Sphere." Hardly pausing after its conquest of Manchuria, the Kwantung army struck south toward Beijing. In China's coastal cities, there were massive boycotts and strikes against Japanese businesses. Japanese marines "protecting" the foreign concession area in Shanghai clashed with Nationalist troops, setting off a ferocious three-month battle in China's largest city. By the spring of 1933, Japanese troops held large sections of Shanghai while far to the north Japan's Manchurian army stood poised for an attack on Beijing and the important ports of Tianjin and Tanggu. Chiang had no choice but to accept a truce worked out by Western diplomats that left Shanghai neutralized and all of China north and east of the Great Wall under Japanese domination.

THE LONG MARCH

Instead of rallying the nation to resist further Japanese aggression, Chiang persisted in viewing the Communist "bandits" as the greatest threat to China's future. He shifted his best troops to the south and mounted an enormous campaign to destroy the Communists in Jiangxi province. His air force bombed the Jiangxi soviet day after day while his army constructed a ring of roads and blockhouses around the Communists' mountain stronghold. By the fall of 1934, the pressure had grown too much for the Communists. The leadership took a desperate gamble. On the night of October 16, the Red Army, led by Marshal Zhu De (1886–1976), broke through the surrounding Nationalist armies and retreated westward in what would become known as the Long March.

**Red Army volunteers crossed hand over hand on the
cables of the Luding Bridge to engage Nationalist guards.**

The Long March is one of the incredible feats in military history. The Red Army suffered hardships almost beyond description. Under almost daily attack by Nationalist troops and planes, the Red Army crossed 24 rivers and hundreds of streams; climbed 18 mountain ranges, some rising as high as 16,000 feet (4,875 m); and slogged through great swamps where a single misstep meant death in the sucking ooze. Often shoeless, canteens and knapsacks empty, the soldiers trudged on, covering mile after mile on their march into the safety of China's vast west and an eternal place in the annals of human courage. In October 1935, after 6,000 miles (9,660 km) and 370 days of almost constant movement, the Red Army set up a new base at Yan'an in remote northern Shaanxi province. Some 80,000 of the original 100,000 soldiers had died on the Long March, but the Red Army had survived. Its example of discipline and dedication awed China and won millions of converts to communism.

The Long March brought Mao to the forefront of the Communist leadership. His brilliant theories of peasant revolution, his iron will, and his unshakeable confidence in the face of disaster made him the dominant member of the leadership circle with Zhu De and Zhou Enlai as his principal allies.

**Tiger Leaping Gorge in Yunnan Province,
one of the obstacles crossed by the Red Army**

DEMANDS FOR RESISTANCE

Chiang's policy of attacking the Communists while allowing the Japanese a free hand in northern China aroused storms of protest. On December 9, 1935, thousands of anti-Japanese students rallied in Tiananmen Square in Beijing. Club-swinging police broke up the demonstration, but the protests spread across China. Nationalist generals demanded the right to fight the invaders. The Communists signaled that they would cooperate in a war against the Japanese. But Chiang remained firm in his policy of fighting the Communists first.

Zhang Xueliang, the "Young Marshal," was among those who disagreed with Chiang's policy. Ordered by Chiang to abandon Manchuria, Zhang had retreated south of the Great Wall to a new base at Xi'an in Shaanxi province. Convinced that Japan was intent on conquering all of China, Zhang favored uniting forces with the Communists. In October 1936, Japanese troops struck south into Suiyuan province, northwest of Beijing, meeting heroic Chinese opposition. A new wave of demonstrations swept China as the people demanded a united front to resist Japanese aggression.

**Chiang Kai-shek and Zhang Xueliang
about the time of the Xi'an Incident**

On December 11, Zhang Xueliang met with his senior officers to set a desperate plan in motion. The next morning, units of Zhang's army stormed Chiang's headquarters outside Xi'an, killing his bodyguards and taking the "generalissimo" captive. Three weeks of complicated negotiations followed as Zhang tried to nail together an anti-Japanese united front. Zhou Enlai flew to Xi'an on December 16 to convince Zhang that only Chiang had the prestige to lead the front. Zhang asked Chiang, but Chiang refused to accept leadership until he was released and flown to safety in Nanjing. To guarantee Chiang's safe passage, Zhang rode the plane to the Nationalists' southern capital. It was an act of remarkable courage, since Zhang knew that he would be entirely at Chiang's mercy once the plane landed. In Nanjing, Zhang was arrested, tried, and sentenced to ten years in prison. Chiang commuted the prison sentence to house arrest but extended the term indefinitely. Only in 1990 was the aged Zhang officially released from house arrest in Taiwan.

JAPAN INVADES

Chiang had little enthusiasm for a united front, but he could no longer ignore the calls for alliance with the Communists. Grudgingly, he agreed to a united front. In the summer of 1937, the Japanese launched an all-out invasion of China. Chinese soldiers fought with astonishing courage, losing 250,000 men killed and wounded in the fight for Shanghai alone, but the Japanese military machine was simply too powerful to defeat. Chiang moved his capital to Hankou, leaving orders for the defense of Nanjing to the last man. But his general fled, and Japanese troops ravaged the city in an orgy of rape, torture, and murder that stunned the world. An estimated 150,000 civilians and captured soldiers died in the infamous "Rape of Nanjing."

**Chinese prisoners were buried alive
during the Rape of Nanjing.**

The immensity of China eventually slowed the invaders. Holding out in Chongqing, Chiang began to receive military aid from the West. But rather than going on the offensive against the Japanese, Chiang hoarded his new equipment for a renewed campaign against the Communists. The Communists were again showing themselves the masters of peasant organization as they built guerilla armies to make hit-and-run attacks on the Japanese across northern and eastern China. Frightened by the growing Communist influence, Chiang ordered the Red Army out of what he claimed as Nationalist territory. In January 1941, Nationalist forces ambushed the Communist New Fourth Army in Jiangxi province, sparking a major battle. After that, Communist and Nationalist forces fought each other almost as often as they fought the Japanese.

The United States declared war on Japan the day after Japanese carrier aircraft struck the United States naval base at Pearl Harbor, Hawaii, on December 7, 1941. While Chinese forces held down two-fifths of the

Japanese army, the United States started the slow process of gaining the offensive against the Japanese Empire. President Franklin D. Roosevelt (1882–1945) dispatched General Joseph "Vinegar Joe" Stilwell (1883–1946) to coordinate operations with Chiang. Stilwell was appalled by the massive corruption and waste in the Nationalist army. He demanded a massive reorganization of the Nationalist war effort and a genuine attempt at cooperation with the Communists. Chiang refused and complained to Washington about Stilwell's arrogance.

After a long contest of wills with Chiang, Stilwell was replaced by a general more sympathetic to the generalissimo. Many of the American military and political experts—including those who had visited Yan'an and gained considerable respect for the Communists—were recalled from China. Meanwhile, Chiang and his American-educated wife became heroic figures to the American press and people. Madame Chiang addressed the United States Congress and toured the country delivering speeches that painted a glowing picture of the heroism, popularity, and good works of the Nationalists. State Department experts who cautioned their bosses that the true picture was not as rosy found themselves transferred to other assignments. In a decision that would cost the United States dearly, the Roosevelt administration put all its hopes in the Nationalists.

World War II ended in August 1945 after the United States dropped two atomic bombs on Japan. Japanese forces in China began a headlong retreat, leaving chaos and devastation behind.

THE COMMUNIST REVOLUTION

Within days of the Japanese surrender, civil war raged in China. Soviet troops seized Manchuria and turned over vast stockpiles of Japanese weapons to Communist troops. The United States airlifted Nationalist soldiers to key cities surrendered by the Japanese while trying to arrange reconciliation between the Nationalists and the Communists. It was hopeless; too many years of bitterness and treachery separated the two sides.

Chiang had lost much of his prestige at home and abroad. The Chinese people, angered by the brutality, corruption, and inefficiency of the Nationalist government, sided more and more with the Communists. Nationalist troops looted everywhere they went while the Red Army held to its strict rules of proper conduct. The nation's economy lay in ruins. Runaway inflation robbed the currency of so much of its value that it literally took an armful to buy the simplest necessity. Flooding in the south destroyed the rice crop, creating famine all over China. Yet the Nationalist government seemed neither willing nor able to do anything to help. For millions of Chinese fighting to survive in a class structure generations old, Mao's policies of seizing the land and wealth of the rich and giving them to the poor seemed to promise a better tomorrow.

Refugees struggle along the flooded Yellow River

After two years of bloody guerilla warfare against the Nationalists, Mao announced that the Red Army was ready to fight Chiang's forces head on. In the early fall of 1948, a brilliant young general, Lin Biao (1908–1971), smashed the Nationalist armies in southern Manchuria. Some 400,000 of Chiang's best troops surrendered or deserted.

Generals Liu Yalou, Lin Biao, and Luo Ronghuan

The Red Army's commander in chief, Marshal Zhu De, ordered Lin Biao to attack the city of Xuzhou on the main railroad line connecting Shanghai and Nanjing with the interior. Against an equal number of Chiang's troops, Lin Biao's 600,000 soldiers were supported in the battle by two million peasant laborers organized by Deng Xiaoping, a senior Party official of great talent who would one day lead a very different revolution in China. After a 65-day pounding, the Nationalist army disintegrated. Lin Biao turned north, capturing Tianjin and receiving the surrender of Beijing on January 31, 1949.

The People's Revolutionary Army enters Beijing.

In the spring and summer of 1949, the Communist armies drove south, routing every Nationalist force in their way. Chiang retreated to the island of Taiwan off the southeast coast, where he would survive under the protection of the United States. On the Mainland, the Communists celebrated their victory by proclaiming the People's Republic of China on October 1, 1949.

Zhengyangmen Gate, Beijing

Chapter 7
The Building of the People's Republic

Huge problems faced the new leaders of China in 1949. For over a century, China had known nearly continuous war and turmoil. The nation had little modern industry, there was terrible poverty in most parts of the country, and most of the outside world was hostile.

As Chairman of the CCP, Mao was the most powerful leader in China. He directed a sweeping series of reforms. The government fixed prices and rationed food and other necessities; took over large businesses and factories; confiscated the land of the rich landlords and began dividing it among the peasants; stockpiled grain in case of famine; expanded education and medical care; began a massive public works program; granted equal rights to women; passed child-labor laws; and instituted a campaign against corruption, opium smoking, and prostitution.

A CONTINUING REVOLUTION

"Revolution," Mao wrote, "is not a dinner party," and the destruction of the class system caused incalculable suffering. Exploited for countless generations, the poor peasants vented their rage in the execution of over a million landlords. Communist officials—called cadres—organized mass meetings of angry workers and peasants to try "reactionaries" who had opposed the revolution. These "people's courts" ordered the execution of hundreds of thousands and sent millions more to labor camps for "reeducation." (Among those "reeducated" was the last emperor, Puyi, who was captured by Soviet troops at the end of World War II and turned over to Communist authorities. Released in 1959, he spent the remaining eight years of his life—apparently quite happily—as a gardener.)

The CCP denounced Confucianism, the philosophy that had been used to justify the old class system. Churches and temples were closed or put under tight government control. Communism and "Mao Zedong Thought" took the place of the old philosophies and religions of China. The leadership began a vigorous campaign to spread the ideology of communism. Schools gave top priority to the teachings of Marx, Lenin, and Mao. Cadres organized mass meetings to educate adults in communism. Newspapers and radio stations became government propaganda organs. The government banned or heavily censored Western books, movies, and plays while directing China's writers and moviemakers to concentrate on telling stories of the glorious revolutionary struggle.

Mao and his wife, Jiang Qing

Anyone who criticized communism or China's leadership risked harsh punishment. The CCP preached the need for "constant vigilance" to protect the revolution from its many enemies: the Nationalist government on Taiwan, the capitalist West, and the old traditions of Chinese life. Under the guidance of the Party, the people must live each day with revolutionary discipline, forever guarding against tendencies to slip back into old ways. Individual liberties of speech, religion, and assembly were examples of "spiritual pollution" from the West and must be rejected for the greater good of the revolution. Even makeup, colorful clothes, and fancy hairstyles were labeled antirevolutionary displays of individuality by the Party.

Yet the CCP had to rein in its revolutionary zeal when it came to rebuilding China's industries and running its large cities. The Guomindang purges of the 1920's and 1930's had largely destroyed the Communist Party in the cities. Few of the rural leaders who had rebuilt the CCP and led it to victory in the revolution had the technical and management skills needed to deal with urban and industrial problems. Tens of thousands of China's best educated and most talented people had fled China as Chiang Kai-shek's government crumbled, and many who remained were unenthusiastic about the Communist takeover. With a shortage of trained experts in its ranks, the CCP was forced to keep many non-Communist managers, professionals, and technicians in their pre-revolution jobs.

THE STRUCTURE OF THE NEW GOVERNMENT

The Communists established a complicated structure to govern the People's Republic of China (PRC). The CCP set all major policies, although to avoid the appearance of one-party rule it allowed the continued existence of a few minor parties. The central government instituted and administered the CCP's policies. The People's Liberation Army (PLA) was assigned the job of protecting the PRC from enemies abroad and from disturbances within while also contributing its vast human resources to large public works projects and rural harvests.

The leadership of Party, government, and army overlapped. Mao was Chairman of the CCP, Chairman of the CCP's Military Commission, and also Chairman of the Central People's Governing Council—a combination that gave him policy control over all three power centers. Zhou Enlai's primary job was supervising the central government as premier of the PRC, but he was also Foreign Minister and had a prominent voice in developing army and CCP policies as a member of the five-person Standing Committee of the CCP's Politburo. Similarly, Zhu De was both commander of the Red Army and another member of the Politburo's Standing Committee. In all, about a dozen officials held similar multiple offices that gave them tremendous power. Although granted the vote by the Chinese constitution of 1949, the people had very little real say in the governing of their country.

THE KOREAN WAR AND A HOSTILE WORLD

The Communist leaders had many reasons to fear for the future of the Chinese revolution. The brief alliance between the Western democracies and the Soviet Union had soured shortly after World War II, leaving the two sides locked in a cold war between capitalism and communism. The Nationalist defeat was considered a monumental disaster by many in the West. Western hard-liners, including some members of the United States Congress, talked of rebuilding the Nationalist armies on Taiwan to "retake China." More practical leaders spoke of "containing communism" within its existing borders.

Chinese soldier killed by U.S. Marines

Korea became the flash point. At the end of World War II, Soviet and American troops had occupied opposite ends of the Korean peninsula. Ignoring repeated requests for free elections in Korea by the newly formed United Nations, the Soviets set up a communist government in the north. On June 25, 1950, communist North Korea invaded republican South Korea. The United Nations approved a "police action" in support of the South. Sixteen nations contributed forces to an army commanded by General Douglas MacArthur (1880–1964) of the United States Army. On September 15, with North Korean troops on the point of complete victory, MacArthur launched a daring amphibious landing at Inchon near the captured South Korean capital of Seoul. Within two months, the Communists were driven back into North Korea.

Meanwhile, President Harry S Truman (1884–1972) sent the United States 7th Fleet to patrol the Taiwan Strait in case the Chinese Communists tried to invade Taiwan while the Western nations were occupied with the war in Korea. The PRC denounced the naval patrols and strenuously objected when UN troops pushed into North Korea in November 1950, seemingly intent on unifying Korea by force. Inflammatory statements by MacArthur of the need for a "second front" on the coast of China by Chiang Kai-shek's army further provoked China's Communist leaders. They began moving hundreds of thousands of troops to China's border with Korea. Some units crossed into North Korea itself. Late in November, as UN troops neared the Yalu River separating Korea from China, the Chinese army struck in overwhelming force. Driven back into South Korea, the UN army rallied again. After more months of heavy fighting, the war settled into a bloody stalemate along the Thirty-Eighth Parallel separating North from South Korea. Infuriated by MacArthur's statements that a second front should be opened with an invasion of China, Truman relieved him in April 1951.

President Truman   **General MacArthur**

Some two million soldiers were killed or wounded by the time an armistice was concluded in July 1953. The bloodshed destroyed any chance for friendly relations between the PRC and the United States or a peaceful reunification of Taiwan and the Mainland. The United States signed a mutual defense treaty with Taiwan and barred the PRC from admission to the UN. It would take nearly two decades for the PRC and the United States to take the first steps toward reconciliation.

THE ELDER BROTHERS

In its isolation from the West, the PRC grew even closer to the Soviet Union. Through the early 1950's, China's leaders urged the people to learn from their "elder brothers": the thousands of advisors sent by the USSR. The PRC patterned its economic, educational, military, and police systems on the Soviet model. The Communist leaders attacked Western influences in China, ending all foreign investment, confiscating most private businesses, and instituting central planning of the economy. Following the Soviet example, the central government issued five-year plans for modernizing the economy. The First Five-Year Plan (1953–57) produced a huge increase in industry and the production of raw materials. The quality of life of hundreds of millions of Chinese benefited as the government conducted campaigns to improve medical care, disease control, literacy, and sanitation.

Mao and Soviet dictator Joseph Stalin

However, the government failed miserably with a series of complicated agricultural reforms. After the revolution, farmers had received shares of the land once owned by rich landlords. Except for harvest and planting times when they worked together in "mutual aid teams," peasant families cultivated their small farms independently. Thanks to the peasants' skill, energy, and traditional love of the land, farm production and income rose sharply. Yet Mao saw a threat to his vision of a classless communist society in private ownership of the land. Before long, he feared, the best and most fortunate of the small farmers would emerge as a new class of rural rich people. At Mao's urging, the CCP chose a new direction for agricultural development.

Peasants harvesting grain

Beginning in 1952, the government started pressuring the peasants to form cooperative farms that could be worked by teams of peasants using modern methods. The plan backfired. Peasants devoted their greatest energies to the small private plots they were allowed to keep, and overall agricultural production fell. Stubbornly holding to its policy, the government expanded the size and number of the cooperatives, but production continued to slide. Deeply frustrated, Mao drafted a new agricultural plan. The government would confiscate all private land and combine the cooperatives into huge collective farms where armies of peasants would work directly under the direction of Party cadres. The Soviet advisors objected, citing the dismal failure of collective farms in the USSR. But to their dismay and the great disappointment of most peasants, Mao rammed his plan through the leadership.

The cooperative farms had been a disappointment; the collective farms were a disaster. Cadres with no experience in farming ordered the wrong crops planted. Expensive machinery ground to a halt for lack of proper maintenance. Peasants, deprived of both land and any sense of independence, worked halfheartedly. Agricultural production plunged.

THE HUNDRED FLOWERS CAMPAIGN

The disaster split the Communist leadership. Opposing Mao were several senior officials who became known as "the pragmatists" since they were more interested in pragmatic solutions to the PRC's economic woes than in elaborate theories of continuing revolution. The pragmatists wanted to streamline the Party and government bureaucracies for the efficient management of a carefully planned series of reforms. Mao, however, saw the emergence of a class of cautious planners and managers as little more than a return to the mandarin system of old China. The policy debate within the Party's inner circle became a power struggle as the pragmatists worked to undercut Mao. Mao fought back by calling for a national debate on China's future: "Let a hundred flowers bloom and a hundred thoughts contend."

By inviting the participation of the people in the debate, Mao expected to prove that the future of communism in China depended not on bureaucratic efficiency but on the revolutionary enthusiasm of the masses. Instead, the Hundred Flowers Campaign revealed a massive distaste for communism as it was being practiced in the PRC. Between May 1 and June 7, 1957, there was a tremendous outpouring of anger. Students and intellectuals led harsh attacks against the CCP, its leaders, and a wide assortment of government policies, particularly the forced collectivization of agriculture. At Beijing University, students plastered a wall with posters demanding individual freedoms and open elections. In some cities, the protests turned violent as people assaulted Party cadres and the system they represented.

Aghast, Mao denounced the flowers as "poisonous weeds." On June 7, the government smashed the movement. Tens of thousands of intellectuals were arrested, labeled "rightists," and sent to prisons or labor camps—some for as long as twenty years. Three student radicals were tried and shot in front of their fellow students. Once again, China lost many of its best-educated and most talented people.

THE GREAT LEAP FORWARD

Mao refused to believe that the intellectuals and students spoke for the people. Instead, he implied that he had engineered the Hundred Flowers Campaign to smoke out rightists thwarting the will of the masses. Marshaling a shaken CCP, he laid out his most radical plan yet for continuing revolution: the Great Leap Forward.

In December 1958, the Central Committee of the CCP ordered the merging of the PRC's 740,000 cooperative and collective farms into 26,000 communes. Some 120 million rural households—99% of the peasant population—would become cogs in the immense machinery of the commune system in which all aspects of individual and family life would be directed by Party cadres. Commune authorities would control the housing, education, medical care, work assignments, recreation, political expression, and even the cooking and eating arrangements of commune members. Couples would have to ask permission to marry or to have a child. Mothers would leave their children in commune day-care facilities while they labored on the land or in one of the thousands of new rural factories. Gigantic armies of peasants would open vast new tracts of farmland, clear forests, and build dikes and roads.

Terraced rice fields, Yunnan Province

The Great Leap Forward has no parallel in human history. Never before had there been an attempt to organize so many people so completely. Several factors made it possible: the Chinese Confucian tradition dictated an acceptance of authority; the suppression of the Hundred Flowers Campaign had silenced nearly all intellectual voices opposed to the CCP and its policies; and—perhaps most important of all—the Communists were utterly ruthless in their indoctrination and organization of the masses. Anyone who questioned, dissented, lingered in obedience, or failed to display anything but enthusiasm for communism and Mao Zedong Thought risked immediate and harsh punishment.

The Great Leap Forward turned into a giant step backward for China. Commune authorities ignored centuries of peasant wisdom as they directed the planting of rice and wheat. The crops failed. When the government ordered a huge increase in steel production, unskilled cadres directed equally unskilled peasants in building a million crude blast furnaces. Peasants gathered every available ounce of scrap metal—some families even contributing their pots and pans—but the furnaces produced unusable slag. Dozens of similar efforts produced similarly shoddy results while frightened cadres tried to hide their blunders with wildly inflated production figures. All the while, China wasted energy and resources at a spectacular rate. Entire forests disappeared under the ax, the wood burned as fuel in a country where good lumber was already scarce. Deforestation caused wind and water erosion that ruined thousands of acres of precious farmland. Torrents of rain rushed unchecked down denuded hillsides, sending rivers boiling over dikes that had protected the land for centuries.

In 1959, Tibetans rebelled against Chinese occupation. The People's Liberation Army suppressed the uprising with a brutality that roused outrage around the world. That same year, the armies of China and previously friendly India clashed in the disputed borderlands between the two nations. Disgusted with Mao and the folly of the Great Leap Forward, the Soviet Union withdrew its advisors in 1960. The Communist superpowers denounced each other for "deviating" from true communism, opening a rift that would last for nearly three decades.

MAO'S POWER EBBS

The troubles abroad added to the deepening crisis in China, where the Great Leap Forward was becoming a disaster of incredible proportions. With grain reserves already at a low point, the weather turned bad and the age-old curse of Chinese life struck: famine. Between 1959 and 1962, an estimated twenty million people—some within an hour's drive of Beijing—starved to death.

Mao largely saw what he wanted to see, but pragmatic Party leaders confronted the disaster. In heated policy debates within the Party's inner circle, the pragmatists argued against Mao's belief that the masses could modernize China with little more than willpower and revolutionary zeal. Premier Zhou Enlai, President Liu Shaoqi (1898–1969), and CCP General Secretary Deng Xiaoping argued that China must place its future in the hands of a new generation of dedicated scientists, technicians, economists, and managers.

Under pressure from the pragmatists, Mao "retired from the front line" to write and think. Although Mao could still exert great influence as Chairman of the CCP, the pragmatists took over management of the economy and the direction of China's modernization. China rebounded from the disaster of the Great Leap Forward. By the mid-1960's, the pragmatists' emphasis on proven methods and careful central (or state) planning reversed the declining standard of living.

DVD case for the documentary *Morning Sun*, perhaps the best film about the Cultural Revolution. In the guard's hand is a copy of *Quotations from Chairman Mao Tsetung*—popularly known as *The Little Red Book*—which became both manual and symbol of the Cultural Revolution.

THE CULTURAL REVOLUTION

Mao watched with increasing frustration as the pragmatists altered his vision of a continuing revolution and a truly classless society. In 1966, he declared the Great Proletarian Cultural Revolution, enlisting an army of young people as Red Guards to overthrow the "revisionists" who were subverting the revolution.

For millions of Chinese, particularly the restless young, the charismatic Mao was still "the Great Helmsman": the intrepid captain who had guided the revolution to victory against the Nationalists. If China had failed to achieve the great hopes of those glorious days, it was only because traitors had wrestled the wheel away from him. When Mao called on the Red Guards to "turn the guns on the revisionist headquarters," they responded with a vengeance.

China's best graphic artists were pressed into service to promote the Cultural Revolution.

The Red Guards accused hundreds of thousands of intellectuals and officials of deviating from Mao Zedong Thought. The accused were beaten, forced to confess to "counterrevolutionary crimes," marched through the streets wearing dunce caps and placards, and then imprisoned or sent to work on communes. Artists, scientists, college professors, doctors, and countless other well-educated people were soon cleaning latrines, slopping hogs, and planting rice. Liu Shaoqi died under house arrest in an isolated city. Deng Xiaoping was sent into rural exile. Only Zhou Enlai had the power and prestige to keep his position.

Over the next several years, the Red Guards persecuted perhaps a 100 million people. Thousands were beaten to death and thousands more committed suicide. Children denounced their parents as "capitalist-roaders." Red Guards broke into homes in search of books, art, and letters that could be considered "counterrevolutionary." In an orgy of destruction intended to rid China of the influence of the past, they burned priceless artworks and manuscripts, defaced ancient shrines, and tore down magnificent buildings dating from the old China.

Lacking central leadership and beyond any restraint, Red Guard factions clashed in bloody street battles. Workers, tired of Red Guard bullying, fought for their factories and neighborhoods. Even Mao was frightened by the huge excesses of the Red Guards. Pressed by Zhou Enlai and others, he began to rein in the violence. The People's Liberation Army took to the streets to restore order.

An English edition of "The Little Red Book"

Lin Biao

THE LIN BIAO PLOT

The PRC's defense minister, General Lin Biao, had stood by Mao in the early 1960's when he had been shunted aside by the pragmatists. Lin had compiled a book, *Quotations from Chairman Mao*, which reinforced Mao's stature as a great leader. In shortened form, it became the "Little Red Book" waved by hundreds of thousands of demonstrating Red Guards. For his loyalty, Mao chose Lin as his successor in 1969.

Lin Biao faced powerful opposition. Premier Zhou Enlai distrusted him and worked to minimize his influence. Radicals led by Mao's wife, Jiang Qing (1914–1991), viewed him as a traitor to the Cultural Revolution for deploying the PLA to control the Red Guards. Lin himself was in a contradictory position regarding a continuation of the Cultural Revolution. He did not want to join Jiang Qing's radical group. However, the Cultural Revolution had served Lin Biao's aims well by driving the pragmatists out of power. Now Premier Zhou Enlai was working quietly to restore a more pragmatic approach to China's problems. If Zhou managed to bring prominent pragmatists back into government, Lin Biao could expect to see his power decline drastically.

If Lin Biao managed to keep in Mao's good graces, he could walk a knife-edge between the pragmatists and the radicals until the aged Mao passed from the scene. But Mao had become suspicious of the ambitious general. Within a year of appointing Lin Biao as his successor, Mao began undermining him. By the late summer of 1971, Lin viewed his situation as critical.

What exactly happened that September is still not entirely clear. Apparently Lin Biao tried a desperate gamble, plotting a military coup and the assassination of Mao. But the plot was uncovered, forcing Lin, his family, and his closest advisors to flee China by air. Interestingly, when Premier Zhou asked Mao if fighter aircraft should pursue Lin's plane, Mao replied with an enigmatic folk saying. Some Western analysts have speculated that Mao saw no reason to reply directly since he had already arranged the sabotage of Lin's plane. Whatever the truth of the matter, Lin Biao never made it to the USSR. En route his plane crashed in Mongolia, killing all aboard.

Mao Mausoleum

Chapter 8
The Pragmatists Triumph

The turmoil of the Cultural Revolution faded slowly. Disenchanted with Mao, more and more people looked to Premier Zhou Enlai as the symbol of stability in China. Zhou had worked diligently behind the scenes to contain the worst of the Cultural Revolution's excesses. He had saved the country's nuclear weapons and defense industries from the Red Guards; maintained critical government services; and protected a number of senior pragmatists, including China's future leader Deng Xiaoping, during their rural exiles.

Following the failed Lin Biao plot, Premier Zhou began quietly arranging the "rehabilitation" of important pragmatists. With the approval of Mao, Deng Xiaoping was appointed executive vice premier, a position that put him in charge of the daily workings of the government. Mao's wife, Jiang Qing, and her fellow radicals bitterly opposed the return of the pragmatists. Hidden from the eyes of the people and most of the rest of the world, a long, complicated struggle began for the future of China.

OPENING TO THE WEST

Mao and Zhou had grown old, their health failing. Yet the two old men had a spectacular trick yet to play. They would end China's long isolation from the world's international affairs.

The diplomatic opening to the West began, strangely enough, with a Ping Pong tournament in Japan. Members of the Chinese and American teams struck up casual friendships during practices. When members of the Chinese team half jestingly invited the American team to visit China, the Americans agreed in the same spirit. When the invitation was reported in the press, Mao and Zhou seized the chance to make the invitation official. In Washington, President Richard M. Nixon (1913–1994) and National Security Advisor Henry Kissinger (1923–   ) had likewise been hoping to open a dialogue. They, too, approved the visit. On April 10, 1971, the United States Table Tennis Team became the first Americans to officially visit China since the revolution.

**American National Security Advisor Henry Kissinger
meets with Premier Zhou Enlai and Chairman Mao Zedong.**

That summer and fall Kissinger made visits—the first in secret—to Beijing to meet with Premier Zhou. Among the world's most skillful diplomats, Kissinger and Zhou negotiated a pair of important events. The first involved China's seat in the United Nations General Assembly and its even more important seat as one of the five permanent members of the UN Security Council. The exiled government of the Republic of China on Taiwan represented China in the United Nations, still claiming that it would one day re-conquer all of China. Although a lifelong anticommunist, President Nixon was far too practical a leader to believe that the Nationalists would succeed. He instructed Kissinger to tell Zhou that the United States would drop its objections to the PRC joining the United Nations. Nixon hoped that better relations with the PRC would help the United States negotiate an end to its frustrating war in Vietnam. Moreover, he hoped that better relations with the United States would discourage the PRC from restoring the close relationship with the Soviet Union the two communist giants had enjoyed in the 1950's.

Kissinger found Zhou receptive, and the United States dropped its opposition to the PRC's claim it should represent China in the UN. The General Assembly voted in favor of the change on October 25, 1971, and the

PRC took China's seat in the Assembly and on the Security Council. At long last, the People's Republic of China had become a member of the world community.

Mao greets President Nixon.

The second major event planned by Kissinger and Zhou came in early 1972 when, to the astonishment of the world, President Nixon flew to China. Nixon had a friendly meeting with Mao and was soon toasting Zhou at a banquet in Beijing's Great Hall of the People. Television coverage of Nixon's visit riveted viewers around the world. After so many years and so many harsh denunciations, the United States and the People's Republic of China had together broken through a great wall of distrust to engage each other in a relationship based not on denunciations but on cooperation.

THE DEATH OF ZHOU

A great outpouring of grief greeted the announcement of Premier Zhou Enlai's death on January 8, 1976. The people had come to view this quiet and wise man as the "elder brother" of all Chinese. At his funeral a week later, Vice Premier Deng Xiaoping delivered a eulogy praising Zhou for his modesty and prudence—virtues that rarely applied to Mao and the radicals. His words sounded, at least to some, like a challenge to Jiang Qing and the radicals. Deng Xiaoping became the target of a renewed campaign by the radicals to discredit the pragmatists.

On April 4, 1976, people all over China prepared for the annual Qingming festival honoring the spirits of ancestors. In Beijing's Tiananmen Square, a large crowd gathered to place wreaths, banners, and placards honoring Zhou at the Monument to the People's Heroes. By the next morning, the police—apparently on the orders of Jiang Qing's radicals—had removed all the tributes. An angry crowd gathered to protest the insult to the memory of Premier Zhou. As the crowd swelled toward 100,000, fighting broke out with police. Demonstrators set police cars on fire and forced their way into government buildings. Most of the crowd went home in the early evening. A few hours later, security forces entered the square in force to disperse the remaining protestors.

Three days later, the Central Committee relieved Deng of all his posts. Following the virtue of prudence he had praised in Zhou, Deng retired to Guangzhou (Canton), where he could expect protection from the region's pragmatic military commander. While Jiang Qing's radicals and Deng's pragmatists maneuvered, a previously obscure politician emerged to become the likely successor to Mao. As a provincial Party chairman, Hua Guofeng (1921–) had carefully courted Mao's favor. Mao responded by naming Hua head of the PRC's public security forces. Jiang Qing's radicals viewed him as a tool, but Hua kept his lines open to the pragmatists. Following Deng's removal as vice premier, Hua became premier and first vice chairman of the CCP, second only to Mao.

DEATH OF THE GREAT HELMSMAN

Mao Zedong, who had shaped the course of one of history's greatest revolutions, died shortly after midnight on September 9, 1976. The death of "the Great Helmsman" roused little of the sorrow that had followed the death of Zhou Enlai. For the Chinese people, Mao had become more the object of awe and fear than of affection. Hua Guofeng became Chairman of the CCP and—at least in title—the most powerful person in China.

Less than a month later, Hua astonished everyone by ordering the arrest of Jiang Qing and three of her main radical allies. The government's mass media let loose a barrage blaming "the Gang of Four" for nearly everything wrong in China. They were tried in 1980, convicted of numerous crimes, and sent to prison for life.

118

Jiang Qing on trial

DENG OUTMANEUVERS HUA

Although Hua had managed to win the PRC's highest positions, he lacked the prestige and talent to hold onto power. Senior military officials demanded the "rehabilitation" of Deng Xiaoping. By July 1977, Deng was again vice premier and exerting great influence in the government. He skillfully outmaneuvered Hua. By 1980, Hua had lost his major titles and was again an obscure member of the Central Committee, where he would continue to serve modestly until his retirement in 2002. That Deng had not ordered Hua's arrest or exile became symbolic of a maturing attitude in Chinese politics. Not every succession dispute had to end in bitterness and utter disgrace for the losing official. Rather, China could accomplish a peaceful succession just like the democratic nations of the West.

Deng Xiaoping

SETTING A NEW COURSE

Much needed to be done to put China back on the path to modernization. Ten years of turmoil and mismanagement during the Cultural Revolution had badly damaged the economy, displaced many of the government's best officials, and nearly destroyed the educational system. Deng laid out a course that would steer China in a very new direction.

During his long years in rural exile, Deng had reached some conclusions about Mao's brand of communism. One of the most important was that China must avoid another "cult of personality" like the one that had grown around Mao. Carefully, he set about cutting Mao's reputation down to size. The CCP issued a new propaganda line, explaining that Mao had fallen out of touch with the people in his old age and made errors under the influence of the Gang of Four. Although China would be forever grateful to Mao for his contributions to the revolution, it was time to move on. Pictures of "the great helmsman" quietly disappeared from most of China's buildings, and references to Mao Zedong Thought became scarce in the media. The position of chairman of the CCP was discontinued, making the general secretary the Party's leading official.

Deng persuaded thousands of elderly Party officials and army officers to retire so that younger people with progressive ideas could advance. He surrendered most of his own positions, nominating younger leaders for the top offices in the CCP and the government. He retained only the chairmanship of the Central Military Commission of the CCP, a position that would give him major behind-the-scenes influence. In 1982, the National Congress of the Chinese Communist Party approved a new constitution, establishing—at least in theory—that henceforth China would be ruled by laws not the whim of strongmen.

THE FOUR MODERNIZATIONS

In 1975, Zhou Enlai and Deng Xiaoping had laid out an ambitious program to modernize national defense, science and technology, agriculture, and industry. During his brief time as premier, Hua Guofeng had pushed ahead with the Four Modernizations through a program of strict central planning and control of the economy.

Deng and his fellow pragmatists had a very different idea of how to achieve the Four Modernizations. Central planning had brought stability and some impressive progress to industry since the disastrous Great Leap Forward in the late 1950's. However, growth rates in nearly all centrally planned economies were modest at best when compared to the growth of free-enterprise economies. In the 1950's, the Soviet Union had boasted that its planned economy would "bury" the West. Instead, the United States and Western Europe were prospering like never before while the Soviet Union and the communist nations of Eastern Europe stagnated. In Asia, Japan, Taiwan, Singapore, South Korea, and Hong Kong were all thriving with their free-market economies. For China's pragmatists, the evidence was clear: China would have to change course.

To put a new economic policy into effect, the pragmatists had first to overcome ideological objections from the left. Jiang Qing and the radicals were safely out of the way, the Cultural Revolution was past, but the stifling commune system remained. Mao's great experiment had tried to change some basic human drives, calling for individuals to set aside personal ambition to work for the good of the group. In reality, however, few people worked very

121

willingly without some hope that their own lives would improve in proportion to how to how much effort they expended.

At the Twelfth Party Congress in 1982, Deng called for "socialism with Chinese characteristics." Instead of following the Soviet example of trying to plan every aspect of the economy, he outlined a "responsibility system" that would allow greater economic freedom for farmers and workers. As part of the plan, he proposed opening free markets for agricultural products and consumer goods. He reassured hard-liners that central planning would remain paramount in the economy with the free markets filling only a secondary role.

Women at work in an embroidery factory

Under the responsibility system, factory work units would fix their own work rules, production quotas, and prices in competition with other factories. Profits—unacceptable in Mao's China—would mean higher wages for workers. Workers who showed special ability and effort would receive bonuses. Critical heavy industries (such as steel, energy, and chemicals) would remain under government control, but Deng's plan permitted people to set up factories in non-essential industries in open competition with government factories producing similar goods.

In the countryside, peasants would no longer labor in large groups on the commune land under the direction of Party cadres. Instead, each family or small groups of families could sign a 15-year lease to farm commune land. They could rent equipment from the commune or buy their own. Part of their crops would go to fill the government quotas, but they could sell any excess on the free market at whatever price they could get. If a few peasants became rich under the new system, so much the better: their success would serve as an example to others.

Selling eels in a free market

When critics complained that the new policy sounded much like capitalism, Deng countered acidly that it made little difference if a cat were black or white as long as it caught mice.

Economic freedom was still heavily restricted by Western standards, but the Chinese people grabbed the new opportunities. In the countryside, the responsibility system stimulated a rapid rise in agricultural production. Free markets sprang up in villages and cities. While keeping many of their old functions in housing, education, and medical care, communes—renamed "townships"—became freer places as people began making more decisions on their own. In the cities, enterprising people—often young people waiting for government job assignments after finishing school—set up restaurants, photography studios, repair shops, and a host of other small businesses. Freed to compete, factories outside of heavy industry became more efficient, their workers motivated by the chance to increase their incomes.

Soldiers of the People's Liberation Army

MODERNIZATION OF THE MILITARY

The pragmatists expected economic growth to provide more money for the modernization of the military. The People's Liberation Army had fallen behind the times in military technology and training. The PLA would buy new weapons, study strategic planning, and adopt new tactics and training. The officer corps would become better educated and more professional, less concerned with political ideology and more with adapting to the demands of modern warfare.

SCIENCE AND TECHNOLOGY

The Cultural Revolution had seriously injured Chinese scientific and technological progress. Despite the efforts of Premier Zhou Enlai to protect scientific research, many scientists were denounced by Red Guards and driven from their laboratories. Universities, high schools, and even middle schools closed down, their students and teachers sent to the countryside to "learn from the peasants." Some students did not return to school for many years, others never had the chance to continue their educations. The waste in human potential cost China untold millions of scientists, engineers, teachers, doctors, and professionals of every category.

Schoolgirls

The pragmatists reopened schools and "rehabilitated" disgraced teachers and scientists. The government initiated a program to upgrade facilities and build new ones. Mao Zedong Thought no longer dominated the curriculum as students learned practical skills that would help China modernize. Thousands of the best students received scholarships for advanced training abroad.

The task of overhauling China's vast educational system couldn't be accomplished overnight. Schools remained crowded and often short of funds. But the unmatched ambition and drive of Chinese students overcame many deficiencies, producing within a decade the largest educated generation in China's history.

ATTRACTING FOREIGN INVESTMENT

In 1979, the government began creating "special economic zones" (SOZ's) in southern coastal regions to attract foreign investment. The PRC would build factories, provide a cheap labor force, and grant low tax rates in exchange for large-scale investment and access to modern manufacturing methods. The industrial nations responded cautiously at first, but soon the zones were prospering.

Deng worked hard to improve ties with the outside world. The PRC and the United States established full diplomatic relations in January 1979. After decades of hostility, the PRC and the USSR began discussions to resolve border disputes. Britain and the PRC signed a treaty that would preserve Hong

Kong's free-enterprise system after the expiration of Britain's 99-year lease in 1997. The reunification of Mainland China and Taiwan remained a thorny issue, but in the new atmosphere of openness, the Communist and Nationalist governments began exchanging ideas through visiting scholars and business travelers. For the first time since the Communist revolution in 1949, overseas Chinese were allowed to visit families in the PRC.

ECONOMIC BOOM

Deng's reforms led to a decade of rapid economic growth. Freed from rigid government control and the daily meddling of local Party and government officials, factories produced a flood of consumer goods. Workers became shareholders with profits reinvested in larger and more efficient factories.

The government removed quotas and price controls from all but a handful of essential goods. With the market determining demand, overproduction fell and products long unavailable or overpriced began appearing on shelves at reasonable cost. Their incomes rising, Chinese consumers scooped up radios, televisions, motorbikes, and a host of other goods in record volumes.

Urban incomes had been twice that of rural areas before reform, but free at last to determine what to plant and how to cultivate their crops, many Chinese peasants were soon earning incomes comparable to city workers'. The commune system had overproduced some agricultural products while keeping others in short supply. The excess had gone into government stockpiles where it often rotted. The free markets corrected the balance, and people were soon enjoying a better and more varied diet.

Before reform, people of all educational levels had been assigned jobs by the government according to what it perceived were the needs of society. The outcome of rigid job assignments was a mismatch of talents to employment for countless millions. Even when some workers performed poorly in unsuitable jobs, no one was fired and few were reassigned. This "iron rice bowl" provided a certain security but it left people with little motivation to work any harder than necessary. Now millions left their old employment for jobs more suited to their tastes. Free to streamline methods and their workforce, manufacturing establishments prospered in the new competitive atmosphere.

At the Thirteenth Party Congress in 1987, the pragmatists refined the system of limited free markets outlined by Deng five years before. Zhao Ziyang (1919–2005), the new general secretary of the CCP, presented a unified plan for economic development. In 1982, Deng had spoken of free market reform as supplementary to central planning. Now Zhao spoke of the free market and central planning as two parts of a "harmonious" whole, essentially making them equal components in economic development. In the future, the government would manage the market through monetary policy and taxation (the methods used in the free enterprise systems of the Western nations), leaving individual enterprises—industrial and agricultural—free to compete in meeting the market's demands.

By 1989, 50% of industry and nearly all of agriculture functioned almost entirely free of central planning. Although heavy industry remained tightly controlled, many industrial plants were introducing the worker incentives that had shown their worth in the free enterprise portion of the economy.

Remnant of a Cultural Revolution poster

BUMPS ON THE PATH TO REFORM

The pragmatists' sweeping economic reforms produced annual growth rates averaging 10% throughout the 1980's. But the figures disguised serious problems as China adjusted to a market economy. The thriving special economic zones (SOZ's) on the coast contributed a disproportionate amount of the growth, leaving inland provinces complaining. In 1987, the Thirteenth Party Congress expanded the number of SOZ's to include some inland areas. But the inland SOZ's would be at a competitive disadvantage until expanded and modernized transportation and power systems could be built.

Improved agricultural production by the household units revealed an overabundance of labor in rural areas. The government pushed a plan to build manufacturing plants in rural areas to employ the excess labor in productive work. By the end of the 1980's, township enterprises were employing nearly 100 million, but another 100 million rural workers remained either unemployed or underemployed. Millions migrated to already overcrowded urban areas in search of work. Despite the new prosperity, there were not nearly enough jobs to absorb the flood of migrants. Crime rates and poverty increased as the migrants huddled in shantytowns on the outskirts. For the first time since the revolution, footloose workers roamed the streets, looking for any job that might offer a day's wage.

Thousands of migrants arrive at Beijing's main railroad station.

The government hoped to slow or even reverse the migration by developing small towns into manufacturing centers with populations of 30,000 to 50,000. To advance this development, it poured money into transportation systems, hydroelectric dams, power plants, and water and sewage facilities. Yet despite this massive investment, much of China remained desperately short of these basic infrastructure improvements.

In the countryside, expensive equipment purchased by the communes for large-scale farming stood unused and rusting. Pollution and the expansion of rural housing and manufacturing destroyed precious farmland. The rural heath system fell into disrepair.

Many factories had been freed of government control, but all too often their managers were former Party cadres with little in the way of managerial training. Some were dishonest, using their positions to siphon off profits. As factories competed for scarce raw materials, managers bribed suppliers or paid outrageous prices, driving up the price of finished products.

The rush to buy manufacturing equipment and consumer products abroad led to a serious trade imbalance and more inflation. The government spent hard currency reserves to pay the trade imbalance, leaving a shortage of funds for the large public works needed to modernize cities and to develop rural manufacturing centers.

Heavy industry and much of manufacturing continued under the tight control of the central government. These inefficient "state-owned enterprises" (SOE's) drained the government's budget of funds desperately needed elsewhere. Industrial workers protested poor working conditions, scarce housing, and low wages. Pollution from coal-burning plants made Chinese cities among the unhealthiest in the world.

In addition to these economic difficulties, the government faced numerous other problems. The population continued to expand at a dangerous rate. Close to a quarter of the people were practically illiterate and hundreds of millions more had only the barest education. Unrest in Tibet led to riots and severe crackdowns by the Chinese authorities. The difficult issue of Taiwan's future continued, complicating the PRC's relations with the United States.

RISING COMPLAINTS

As economic problems grew, Deng Xiaoping and the pragmatists came under increasing criticism. Hard-liners in the inner circles of the Party and the government complained that China had lost sight of the goals expressed in Mao Zedong Thought. Advocates of central planning warned that the government must restore controls to prevent a meltdown of an overheated and wasteful economy. Military leaders complained that their "modernization" had received too little attention.

Under pressure to rein in reform, Deng and the pragmatists had worries enough. They would shortly to have more as the spring of 1989 brought warm weather to Beijing. China's students, agents of so much change in the past, were about to give voice to the demand for a fifth modernization: democracy.

Tiananmen Square, 1989

Chapter 9
The Democracy Movement

The pragmatists' daring economic reforms in the 1980's unleashed a flood of individual economic initiative. Even with the problems encountered along the way, progress had been spectacular. By 1989, many Chinese, particularly students and intellectuals, were asking if similar political reforms might not produce similarly beneficial results.

Economic reform had required some loosening of control over the lives of the common people. Yet most civil rights common in the West were unknown in China. Government officials still decided where people lived, what they could read, watch or listen to, how long they continued in school, when a couple could marry, how many children they could have, and on down a long list of decisions that people in the West made for themselves. Political power was exercised entirely by senior members of the Party. Anyone who spoke out against the CCP or communism itself did so at great personal risk. Punishments ranged from public criticism, to loss of job and privileges, to "reeducation" in a labor camp, to imprisonment, and finally—for the worst offenders—to public execution.

THE OBLIGATION OF AN EDUCATION

Students and intellectuals knew the risks of challenging the CCP, but they persisted in their advocacy of civil rights and democracy. Since the time of the first scholar-mandarins, people who sought higher educations in China accepted special patriotic and moral obligations. In exchange for the great respect granted them by society, they were obligated to use their knowledge in the service of the country. When China strayed from the path of harmony and justice, it was their moral obligation—freely sought and willingly accepted—to speak out whatever the risks to livelihood, family, personal freedom, or life itself.

Time and again, Chinese intellectuals paid a terrible price. In old China, outspoken scholars were banished, tortured, and hanged on the order of emperors. As the dynastic system rotted, intellectuals formed underground societies to search for ways to save China. But time and again, imperial secret police smashed their organizations.

In 1898, the intellectuals nearly succeeded in reforming the old system when they engineered the Hundred Days Reform, but the Empress Dowager Cixi crushed the movement and imprisoned the liberal young emperor,

Guangxu. In the early 20th century, scholars and students helped overthrow the last dynasty and spearheaded attempts to establish a republic in China, only to be disappointed as warlords and foreign meddling destroyed the Dr. Sun Yat-sen's fragile republic. Yet they did not give up.

The May 4th Movement

On May 4, 1919, students in Beijing launched a crusade to strengthen China. The May 4th Movement produced a flood of books, pamphlets, and essays calling for the end of warlord rule and foreign interference in China's affairs, the organization of unions, women's participation in public life, and the rejection of Confucian dogmatism in favor of new political ideologies. Responding to calls for a new patriotism, multitudes of students joined political movements. Most students favored the democratic socialism of Dr. Sun Yat-sen's Guomindang (Nationalist) party. But many others chose to join the recently formed Chinese Communist Party.

China's students and young intellectuals were among the most dedicated and selfless warriors on both sides in the titanic struggle that ended with the defeat of the Nationalists and the triumph of communism in 1949. But in the PRC established by Mao, the students found themselves shunted to the political sidelines. They were expected to study hard, to work for the advancement of the people, and otherwise to keep quiet while the Communist leadership determined the course ahead.

Silence did not come easily to the students. They spoke out in the debates of the brief Hundred Flowers Campaign in the mid-1950's and suffered the consequences. Misled by the charismatic Mao, they abandoned their books and took to the streets in the Cultural Revolution of the 1960's and 1970's. The students were not always right, as the excesses of the Cultural Revolution proved, but they always had passion and an overwhelming desire to speak out. In the struggle between hard-liners and pragmatists following the death of Mao, they were ready to do so again.

THE DEMOCRACY WALL MOVEMENT

In November and December 1978, students plastered a wall near Beijing's Forbidden City with posters, poems, and essays calling for democratic reform. Wei Jingsheng, a young intellectual, became the leading speaker for the movement when he posted an essay arguing that democracy was "the fifth modernization," without which all the rest were meaningless. The Democracy Wall inspired similar walls in other cities and demonstrations for civil rights in Beijing, Guangzhou, and Shanghai.

Wei Jingsheng

The students may have been morally correct, but their timing was terrible. Little more than two years had passed since the death of Mao. The Gang of Four had yet to stand trial. Deng Xiaoping and the pragmatists had only recently returned to positions of power in the government and the Party. Hard-liners opposed the pragmatists' plans to overhaul the economy. Within the pragmatic leadership, considerable doubt remained about what programs would or would not work. For Deng and the pragmatists, it was time for careful economic experimentation, not for a headlong plunge into democracy.

Like the hard-liners, the pragmatists were dedicated members of the CCP, convinced that the Party alone should chart China's future. For a few months they let the students express themselves with minimal interference. But in March 1979, Deng made a speech putting stern limits on the Democracy Wall Movement.

Wei Jingsheng fearlessly responded by posting an essay warning the Chinese people that Deng was becoming dictatorial and calling for a general election. Wei was immediately arrested. To avoid the appearance of arbitrarily suppressing speech, the authorities allowed the Democracy Wall Movement to continue for a few months under strict controls. Meanwhile, Wei was convicted of treason and sent to prison. (Released in 1993, Wei would soon resume his political activities. Rearrested a year later, he would be released at the personal request of President William J. Clinton (1946–) and allowed to emigrate to the United States in 1997, where he continues to speak out for democracy in China.

RUMBLINGS

Over the next few years, the Communist leadership kept the lid on protests and calls for democracy. As every authoritarian regime understands, control of the mass media is vital to control over dissent. But rising living standards in the 1980's put televisions and radios in the hands of many more Chinese. Broadcasts from Hong Kong, Taiwan, and Japan brought a steady flow of information and images showing the material well-being and political freedom enjoyed by people in the democratic nations. Visiting overseas Chinese described a world that, for all its faults, was immensely freer than the PRC.

In December 1986, seven years after the crushing of the Democracy Wall Movement, renewed protests for democracy, better living standards, and an end to official corruption broke out in Beijing, Shanghai, and a half dozen other cities. The government moved quickly to suppress the protests, disciplining outspoken intellectuals and arresting the movement's ringleaders, who were accused of spreading the "spiritual pollution of decadent capitalism." Among those singled out were the prominent scientist Fang Lizhi (1936–) and the popular writer Liu Binyan (1925–2005). Hu Yaobang (1915–1989), the pro-reform general secretary of the CCP, was made a scapegoat for the unrest and dismissed from office.

The imposed silence did not last long. Late in 1988, as the PRC prepared to celebrate its fortieth anniversary, some of the nation's most prominent writers and scientists wrote letters to Deng Xiaoping. They suggested that he use the anniversary for a radical overhaul of the CCP and the opening of the government to participation by China's masses. Deng, beset with problems in the economy, harshly dismissed the intellectuals' pleas.

On April 15, 1989, the popular Hu Yaobang died. Student leaders used the occasion to organize memorials to Hu and demonstrations for better schools, an end to corruption, the release of political prisoners, and the beginning of democratic reform. They spread their call for action through wall posters, leaflets, fax machines, and computer networks. Word of mouth did the rest.

Tiananmen Square

TIANANMEN SQUARE

The demonstrations that the world would identify with the great public square at the heart of Beijing began on April 17, 1989. That morning, thousands of students poured into Tiananmen Square to put flowers and posters beneath a large portrait of Hu Yaobang placed on the Monument to the People's Heroes. Throughout the day, student groups marched to the monument, where they listened to speeches, sang revolutionary songs, and chanted slogans calling for reform within the Communist system.

The next day an even larger crowd assembled in the square. A student leader climbed the monument to read a list of demands through a bullhorn. The crowd cheered the calls for freedom of speech and assembly, a larger education budget, a reevaluation of Hu Yaobang's contribution to the PRC, and a new openness by China's leaders. It seemed mild stuff by Western standards, but the demands and the crowd's reaction represented a direct challenge to the Communist leadership. In an act of unprecedented bravado, several hundred students began a sit-in near the entrance of the Great Hall of the People. Several thousand more demonstrated in front of the Zhongnanhai, the walled compound west of the square where many Communist leaders lived, demanding an audience with Premier Li Peng (1928–   ).

**Monument to the People's Heroes,
Mao's Mausoleum in the background**

MASS PROTEST

The protest dwindled on April 20 when only a few hundred demonstrators braved a heavy rain. But when sunshine returned on April 21, 100,000 demonstrators poured into the square. In some two hundred cities across China, people gathered by the tens of thousands to show their support for the Beijing demonstrations. The next day, as officials gathered for Hu's memorial services in the Great Hall of the People, an estimated 200,000 people gathered in the square to demand a dialogue with the leadership.

The students hoped to win the attention of Zhao Ziyang, Hu Yaobang's successor as general secretary of the CCP and a leader considered more flexible than Deng Xiaoping or the hard-line Li Peng. But Zhao and the leadership remained silent, hoping that the demonstrations would fade after Hu's memorial services. Instead, the protests spread. Students across China went on strike, many of them forming independent unions in a direct challenge to the law forbidding the formation of any organization not approved by the CCP.

On April 26, the *People's Daily*, the CCP's official newspaper, labeled the democracy movement "a planned conspiracy [to] throw society into chaos and destroy the peaceful united political system." The warning backfired. The next day saw the biggest demonstration yet as 250,000 people marched into central Beijing. Thousands of workers left their factories to help the students force their way through police barricades surrounding the square. Delegations of army officers, newsmen, and government officials joined the march to show their support for changes in the system.

THE GOVERNMENT SOFTENS

Confronting a protest movement that was growing rather than fading, government leaders agreed to meet with student leaders. The talks went nowhere. The government refused to recognize the independent student unions, and the students refused to negotiate until it did. On May 4, the 70th anniversary of China's most famous protest movement, 100,000 chanting, sign-waving students marched down the broad streets leading to the square. In a gesture part irony, part plea, they sang the words of the Chinese national anthem as they passed the Zhongnanhai compound: "Rise ye who refuse to be slaves."

For a week after the May 4 march, both sides backed away from confrontation. Zhao Ziyang delivered a speech to foreign bank officials that seemed to promise that the government would address the protestors' concerns. Most of the students returned to classes. But the quiet was deceptive as the capital prepared for a long-anticipated event.

THE GORBACHEV VISIT

Deng Xiaoping had carefully orchestrated a warming of relations with the USSR after nearly thirty years of hostility. To signify the new friendship between the Communist giants, Deng invited Soviet General Secretary Mikhail Gorbachev (1931–) to visit Beijing in the middle of May.

The students awaited Gorbachev's visit with open enthusiasm. The smiling, progressive Gorbachev had relaxed Soviet control over Eastern Europe and initiated a policy of economic and political reform in the USSR. Chinese leaders appealed to the students to refrain from demonstrations during Gorbachev's visit, but on May 13 students again gathered in Tiananmen Square. Some 3,000 put on white headbands and began a hunger strike. By the time Gorbachev flew into Beijing two days later, thousands of students were sleeping in the square. During the day, crowds swelled to well over 100,000. Deeply embarrassed, the government shifted welcoming ceremonies for Gorbachev from the Great Hall of the People to the airport.

On May 16, the crowd in the square numbered several hundred thousand. Chinese officials whisked Gorbachev through a back door into the Great Hall of the People for a meeting with Deng Xiaoping and other senior leaders. Outside in the square, the festive mood of the crowd was dampened as hundreds of hunger strikers collapsed and were rushed to hospitals. Chinese newspapers and television stations ignored government censorship to report the condition of the hunger strikers. Shortly after midnight, Zhao Ziyang sent a message from the Politburo Standing Committee promising "concrete measures to enhance democracy." In return, he begged the protestors to return to their schools and jobs. His plea went unheeded as students and their sympathizers demonstrated in cities across China.

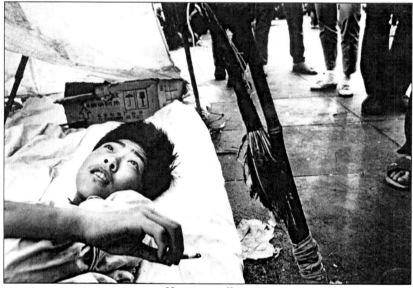

Hunger striker

THE ASTONISHING 17TH

At dawn on the morning of May 17, 1989, more than a million demonstrators marched toward Tiananmen Square. Factory workers, peasants, government employees, intellectuals, journalists, and even soldiers and police joined the flood. Thousands of banners, many carrying the inscriptions of newly formed independent student, craft, and labor unions, waved above the marchers. Foreign television crews beamed the incredible scene to an astonished world.

On May 18, as a bemused Gorbachev left China, a million people again gathered in the square. In the aftermath of what should have been a public relations triumph, the Chinese leadership faced a desperate choice: world condemnation if they called in the army or the possible destruction of the Communist system if they gave in to the demonstrators' demands. Premier Li Peng met with student leaders but neither side would give in.

Still smiling, young soldiers push through the pleas of the strikers.

In the predawn of May 19, Zhao Ziyang visited the hunger strikers, tearfully apologizing for coming so late. He begged them to end their fast, but most refused. By day's end, some 2,400 of the 3,000 strikers were hospitalized. Zhao tried to find support for compromise within the Communist leadership. But Deng Xiaoping backed Li Peng and the hard-liners in a declaration of martial law.

On May 20, troop convoys rumbled into the outskirts of Beijing. In street after street crowds chanting "patriotism is no crime" blocked their way. Most of the soldiers knew little of the Democracy Movement and expected to find "hooligans" disrupting the city. Instead, they saw Chinese of every age and every walk of life peacefully protesting for change. Citizens brought them drinking water and explained their protests to the young soldiers. As the soldiers' loyalty began to waver, officers hastily pulled the convoys back.

STANDOFF

Giving into pleas from other protestors, the hunger strikers gave up their fast on May 20. Three days later, a million demonstrators marched through the streets of Beijing, demanding Li Peng's resignation and the retirement of Deng Xiaoping.

The students' round-the-clock occupation of Tiananmen Square entered its second week. To pass the time, the students played music, danced, and engaged in endless debates about the form a Chinese democracy should take. Many exhausted Beijing students went back to their dormitories and apartments to recover, but thousands of fresh students from universities across China took their place.

Some Beijing art students hit on the idea of providing the protest with a symbol. They erected a 33-foot (10-m) plaster and Styrofoam figure of a young woman holding a torch above her head, somewhat reminiscent of the Statue of Liberty in America's New York harbor. "The Goddess of Democracy" became the rallying point for the students holding doggedly to the square.

PRELUDE TO TRAGEDY

Paralyzed a week before, the government was now firmly in the hands of the hard-liners. The increased participation of workers in the demonstrations had tipped the scales. Students might put down their books for a few weeks and shout themselves hoarse without doing real damage. But workers organized into independent trade unions represented a deadly threat to the Party's power.

Some 200,000 troops surrounded Beijing. In the early morning hours of June 3, army convoys entered the Beijing suburbs. Crowds streamed into the streets of the working-class neighborhoods surrounding the square. Pledging to defend the students, they blocked intersections with barricades of buses and concrete traffic barriers. Some convoys withdrew; others sat stalled as a hot day dawned. Occasional scuffles broke out, but student leaders hurried to intervene, insisting that the demonstrators remain peaceful. Yet push was coming rapidly to shove. About 2:00 P.M., soldiers and riot police stormed out of the Zhongnanhai, firing tear gas and swinging riot sticks. The crowd drove them back with rocks and clubs.

MASSACRE

As night fell, the army's convoys still sat stalled a mile from the square. Crowds had blocked the largest column with a barricade of buses at the Gongzhufen intersection on a wide thoroughfare that becomes Changan Boulevard about a mile from the southwest entrance to Tiananmen Square. About 10:30 P.M., twenty armored personnel carriers charged the barricade. They smashed through, crushing demonstrators under their tracks. Firing machine guns, the personnel carriers roared through the working-class neighborhood along the boulevard. The crowds fought back with rocks, firebombs, and clubs, slowing the column.

The course of the fighting over the next four hours is almost impossible to trace. Several army columns converged on the square, all at least temporarily halted by barricades and worker resistance. Some troops abandoned their vehicles rather than fire on the people, and crowds set fire to dozens of empty trucks and personnel carriers. A number of soldiers were waylaid and beaten to death, but students and workers who risked their own lives rescued many more.

Students rescue a wounded soldier

Most of the bloodshed occurred along Changan Boulevard as the main assault plowed through barricades and crowds, leaving thousands of civilians dead or wounded. Soon hospitals and morgues overflowed with casualties from the massacre along "bloody boulevard."

THE RETAKING OF TIANANMEN

A few thousand resolute students waited in Tiananmen Square. The dull light of burning buses and army vehicles glowed beyond the Great Hall of the People. Tracer bullets arced over Mao's tomb as they gathered beneath the Goddess of Liberty, linked hands, and sang.

About 2:00 A.M. on June 4, the army broke through to the square. Eyewitness accounts of the next three hours vary widely. Apparently, the troops took positions around the square to await further orders. Police officers isolated foreign journalists, arresting a few and demanding film and videotapes from the others. A crowd of students marched toward the soldiers to show their defiance. With or without orders, some soldiers fired, killing at least a few students and perhaps many more.

At 4:00 A.M., the lights around the square went out. Fearing an all-out attack, the rock star Hou Dejian begged officers for time to let the students leave in peace. At 4:30 A.M., the lights came back on, and a government loudspeaker announced that the students could go. Most of the students agreed to leave. Singing the *Internationale*, the old song of world revolution, they marched down a corridor of soldiers and out the southeastern entrance to the square. But outside they ran into an army column apparently unaware of the agreement. The lead tank charged, crushing perhaps ten students and sending the others fleeing. Panicked soldiers opened fire, cutting down many more.

Inside the square, an armored personnel carrier toppled the Goddess of Democracy. Other personnel carriers methodically destroyed the students' camp. Student leaders later claimed that dozens—perhaps hundreds—of students waiting to surrender were crushed inside the tents. Bulldozers pushed the debris into a huge bonfire at the center of the square. A tall column of oily smoke rose into the Beijing morning.

AFTERMATH

It took the army several days to restore order in Beijing and some eighty cities across China. The government began widespread arrests. The outspoken scientist Fang Lizhi and his wife sought refuge inside the United States embassy. Other protest leaders escaped abroad, but most were imprisoned. Thousands of students were hustled off to "reeducation" camps.

The government imposed a ban on independent news reporting. Only a fragmentary picture of the massacre reached the outside world. Most reporters and television crews had seen only the chaos in Tiananmen Square, and few stories reported the heavy fighting in the working-class neighborhoods along

Changan Boulevard. Spokesmen for the Chinese government downplayed the violence, blaming "hooligans and counterrevolutionary elements" for the "incident." Understandably, the student leaders who survived tried to paint the government in the worst possible hues.

An unknown artist posted this caricature of the CCP leadership.

How many were killed or injured may never be known. Estimates range from 300 to 3,000 killed and from 6,000 to 30,000 injured. Military and civilian police arrested at least 30,000 people and perhaps tens of thousands more. Courts were particularly savage in dealing with workers. Of the approximately sixty leaders executed, most were workers.

Li Peng and the hard-liners took control of the government. Across China, millions of people were subjected to "reeducation" in their schools and communities. After years of declining power, Party cadres again watched for the least deviation from the "party line." Zhao Ziyang was relieved of his posts and placed in house arrest. Deng Xiaoping resigned the last of his posts and retired from public view. Parroting the CCP's propaganda when they had to, whispering of a better tomorrow when they could, the Chinese people—their brief spring of exuberant freedom extinguished—settled in to wait for the next turn in the long cycle of Chinese history.

Tibetan woman at prayer

Chapter 10
Hard-liners and Pragmatists

The first horrifying pictures of fire and carnage in Tiananmen Square shocked people around the world. Most of the world's democracies condemned China's leaders, but the outcry diminished quickly as governments became concerned that denunciations might do more harm than good.

The democracies faced a dilemma in choosing the best way to promote political change in China. Since the 1970's, China had become an increasingly important diplomatic and military power. By inviting foreign investment and trade, the pragmatists had taken a major step toward increasing the living standards of hundreds of millions of Chinese. Yet China's ties with the outside world were fragile. Many foreign leaders in government, business, and intellectual circles argued that trade, investment, and quiet diplomacy could do more for the long-term benefit of the Chinese people than economic sanctions and harsh criticism of China's leadership. In a world struggling to find peace and stability, no one wanted to see China choosing isolation again.

President George H. W. Bush (1924–   ), a former United States ambassador to Taiwan, directed a carefully non-confrontational policy toward the PRC. Only weeks after the massacre, National Security Advisor Brent Scowcroft (1925–   ) flew to Beijing to assure the Chinese leadership of America's continued interest in building diplomatic and economic ties. Bush vetoed a Congressional bill granting permanent resident status to pro-democracy Chinese students studying in the United States, but extended the students' visas by executive order. The administration imposed a few largely cosmetic trade sanctions, but—to the great disappointment of democratic activists—rejected calls for suspending diplomatic and trade relations. At the request of the Bush administration, the PRC gave permission for Fang Lizhi and his wife to leave China. He settled in the United States where he continues to speak out for human rights and democracy in China.

COLLAPSE OF THE SOVIET EMPIRE

The world's attention was drawn away from China by dramatic events in Eastern Europe. In the amazing fourteen months following Tiananmen Square, the Soviet Empire in Eastern Europe collapsed. Allowed to choose their own future by Soviet General Secretary Gorbachev, Poland, Czechoslovakia, Hungary, East Germany, Romania, and Bulgaria threw out their Communist regimes and sent Soviet troops home. By the late summer of 1990, only fragmenting Yugoslavia and tiny Albania still had communist governments.

President-elect George H. Bush, President Ronald Reagan and Soviet General Secretary Mikhail Gorbachev in 1988

The massive rejection of the communist system spread to the Soviet Union itself. Gorbachev tried to hold the USSR together. But, by the second anniversary of Tiananmen Square, most of the Soviet republics were demanding self-government. In August 1991, Soviet hard-liners put Gorbachev under house arrest and took over the government. The people of Moscow stormed into the streets by the hundreds of thousands to resist the coup. Refusing to fire on their fellow citizens, Soviet troops joined the demonstrators. Boris Yeltsin (1931–2007), president of the Russian Republic, mounted a tank to demand the ouster of the hard-liners. The coup leaders surrendered, and the people celebrated the triumph of democracy in Russia.

Over the next few months, the Soviet Union broke apart as its member states reasserted sovereignty over their affairs. Gorbachev was shunted to the sidelines. The collapse of the Soviet Union left the PRC as the only remaining Communist power. As even the hard-line regimes in Albania and the Mongolian People's Republic moved toward democracy, only Cuba, North Korea, and China held firmly to the communist line.

Russian President Boris Yeltsin with President William Clinton

ROLLING BACK ECONOMIC REFORM

With Deng Xiaoping in retirement after Tiananmen, Premier Li Peng restored price controls to a number of commodities, raised interest rates to reduce inflation, and stopped government loans to private enterprises. He attempted to roll back other market reforms in favor of stronger central planning but was thwarted by Jiang Zemin (1926–   ), Zhou Ziyang's successor as general secretary of the CCP.

While taking a backseat to the hard-liners, the pragmatists argued that recent problems in the economy did not negate the remarkable progress made by the economy in the 1980's. The pragmatists admitted that there might be some truth to the hard-liners' denunciations blaming Western influences for crime, corruption, and a decline in morals and respect for authority. But they argued that a return to the days of tight social and economic controls would only delay China's emergence as a modern superpower. Instead, China should pursue Western economic methods while preserving Communist control.

Jiang Zemin

Although Deng Xiaoping no longer held official positions, he continued to exercise influence in the inner councils of the government. Li Peng recognized that he could not curtail reform entirely without denouncing Deng, a step that would open a vicious struggle within the leadership. He settled for what conservative policies he could get. When the aging Deng passed from the scene, he would try for more against Jiang Zemin and the pragmatists.

Some of Li Peng's policies were overdue. Reducing inflation, controlling the migration of rural workers to urban areas, and devoting more money to infrastructure development would all provide long-term benefits for the economy. After a period of stabilization, the economy would be ready for another surge.

DENG'S SOUTHERN EXPEDITION

For more than a year, Deng Xiaoping remained out of public view. In January 1992, he judged the time right to make a dramatic statement about the future of China. He set out on his famous "Southern Expedition," a phrase reminiscent of the southern tours once undertaken by Chinese emperors. He visited the Shenzhen Special Economic Zone, a sleepy village transformed by economic reform into a booming city where ultramodern skyscrapers rose above the green countryside of Guangdong Province and the blue waters of the South China Sea. In a series of speeches, Deng praised the free market and criticized the hard-liners for clinging to their belief in central planning. "A planned economy is not equivalent to socialism," he announced. Where the free market produced better results, central planning should be discarded to better advance the "ultimate achievement of prosperity for all."

Shenzhen Special Economic Zone

To Western ears, Deng's pronouncements seemed tame, even boring stuff. To the Chinese they were hugely significant. Economic central planning was a basic principle of Marxist-Leninism and Mao Zedong Thought. Deng Xiaoping and the pragmatists, for all their progressive thinking, had maintained the principle through the early years of reform. In 1982, the Twelfth National Party Congress had been careful to emphasize that the newly created free market was only a supplement to central economic planning. Five years later, the Thirteenth National Party Congress had put the two on an equal footing by declaring them parts of a "harmonious" whole. Now Deng was saying that the proportion of the two didn't matter as long as the right method was chosen to advance economic progress. If that meant that central planning might eventually be discarded entirely, so be it. Let economic reform "blaze a trail and press forward boldly."

Deng and President Jimmy Carter

THE REACTION

It is hard to underestimate the daring of Deng's declarations. In the past, his policies had frequently enraged strict adherents to Mao Zedong Thought. A reported seven times in his career he had been the target of assassination attempts. Now he was announcing what amounted to a redefinition of communism and a radically new vision of China's future.

To the hard-line leaders in Beijing, Deng's speeches were not only a direct challenge to their leadership but an assault on the system they had spent their lives building. Desperate for time to formulate a counterattack, the hard-liners tried to keep Deng's views out of the media. But when Deng wrote a series of articles under a thinly disguised pseudonym, the media threw off government censorship and spread the story across China. The effect was electric. Public sentiment landed squarely in Deng's corner. The army signaled its approval. The pragmatists, who had been carefully maneuvering to reassert power, spoke out boldly. By the time the Fourteenth Party

Congress met in March of 1992, the pragmatists had gained control of the debate. Deng laid out his plan in detail, winning approval for the radical step of abandoning central planning in favor of a "socialist market economy."

Deng Xiaoping had outmaneuvered the hard-liners in the supreme triumph of his long, eventful life. Li Peng suffered a heart attack in the spring of 1993. Although he would remain premier for another five years, much of his power shifted to a newly appointed vice premier, the pragmatic and gifted Zhu Rongji (1928–). Jiang Zemin established himself as China's preeminent leader by adding the post of president to his list of offices. With Deng's backing and inflation under control, he loosened Li Peng's policies.

The economy revived quickly and roared ahead. Soon growth in the gross national product and living standards exceeded that of the 1980's. In the four years following Deng's Southern Expedition in 1992, China's GNP increased by nearly 13% per year before falling to a still very impressive 8% per year through the rest of the decade. China erased its negative trade balance, accumulating a surplus of nearly $25 billion annually from 1994 to 1999. Household incomes grew at an estimated 7% annually when adjusted for inflation.

A Sunday market in Kashgar, Xinjiang Province

THE HUMAN COST

The mid-1990's brought the most radical restructuring of Chinese society since the establishment of the commune system during the Great Leap

Forward forty years before. The central government abandoned many of the functions it had performed under Mao, transferring the responsibilities for education, welfare, and health care to local governments. Short of money and expertise, the local governments had difficulty assuming the burden, and all three areas suffered, particularly in the countryside. Taxation was pegged at 5% of farmers' incomes, but new fees and assessments added considerably to what the farmers had to pay. Dishonest cadres grew rich on fraudulent surcharges as corruption spread at every level of government.

Local schools, under-funded in the best of times, ran short of teaching materials, qualified teachers, and money to modernize facilities. Government spending on education was a paltry 2.5% of gross national product, a figure exceeded by more than a hundred other nations. Many poorer families took their children out of school altogether rather than pay the new fees. The tradition of keeping girls at home to work while boys went to school reasserted itself among many of the rural poor.

Only one fifth of government health spending was devoted to providing care for the rural population. Rural health facilities suffered from a lack of funds, equipment, and medical personnel. Even people with the means to pay clinic and hospital fees often faced long delays unless they could afford to bribe their way to higher places on waiting lists. The system of "barefoot doctors" that had provided basic health care under the commune system was abolished without adequate replacement. Prenatal and child medical care were particularly affected by the imposition of the socialist market economy on health care.

For all its faults, the commune system had at least guaranteed a job and a minimum living standard for all. Under the rural responsibility system, many common people struggled to find adequate employment and income. The dream of every farmer prospering on his own patch of leased land proved impossible because of the overabundance of labor and the scarcity of productive soil. Many peasants were forced to work for those fortunate enough to hold the best land. Old resentments forgotten in the era of collective farming began reasserting themselves in many communities.

The reformers had hoped that the responsibility system would narrow the difference between rural and urban incomes. But after a brief surge in agricultural incomes, the gap increased substantially. In 2000, annual rural incomes averaged $272, urban incomes $743. With the difference in access to health, welfare, and education figured in, the disparity was even greater.

THE URBAN POOR

All was hardly rosy in the cities either. Thousands of state-owned enterprises found themselves unable to compete in the socialist market economy. Between 45 and 60 million industrial workers—a third of the urban labor force—lost their jobs when the government closed, sold, or consolidated SOE's. Between 1990 and 2000, the number of large and medium-sized SOE's declined from 100,000 to 65,000. No longer guaranteed lifelong employment—the so-called "iron rice bowl"—laid-off workers had to seek new jobs, often at reduced wages and benefits.

Urban unemployment swelled as millions of rural folk moved to the cities where they joined laid-off industrial workers in a search for work. Under the commune system the government had maintained strict control of where people lived and worked. The replacement of the commune system by the rural responsibility system had rendered at least 200 million rural workers excess. The local manufacturing enterprises established in the countryside absorbed half the number but soon ran into trouble. Untrained labor and inexperienced management often produced goods of poor quality that couldn't compete in the global market. Foreign banks and companies preferred to invest in the thriving special economic zones in coastal provinces where more advanced manufacturing and transportation systems provided better business conditions. Growth of the local enterprises slowed, leaving many rural workers with little choice but to migrate to the already overcrowded cities. By the year 2000, some 100 million rural workers had permanently resettled in the cities. Social services in the cities groaned under the burden, often providing little or no help for rural migrants or laid-off urban workers. Crime, including the old ills of prostitution and drug addiction, prospered in the slum areas populated by the increasing number of urban poor. HIV/AIDS spread at an alarming rate while the government initially refused to acknowledge the problem. Dishonest job contractors exploited the poor, often paying late or not at all. Police harassed slum dwellers. Poor families had difficulty placing their children in urban schools or finding health care.

When looked at as a national total, incomes rose at a healthy rate in the 1990's, but millions of workers and farmers found the opposite happening in their personal lives. Looking about them, they could see luckier people—particularly members of the new middle class—living better than ever before. Government officials likewise seemed better off. Exactly when would economic reform benefit all the people? Talk of the "rich getting richer and the poor getting poorer" became part of an undercurrent of resentment among those who had yet to share in China's economic good times.

Skyscrapers in the Shenzhen Special Economic Zone

TURNING THE MILLENNIUM

In one of his most famous pronouncements Mao said, "Revolution is not a tea party." Although the economic revolution in China in the 1980's and 1990's was not as violent or as traumatic as the Maoist revolution of the first two decades of Communist rule in China, it was in many ways as profound. The upsetting of the commune system destroyed many of the social guarantees promised by Mao's brand of communism. The economic revolution formulated and carried out by Deng Xiaoping and the pragmatists upset a system that, for all its faults, provided a large measure of security. The imposition of the socialist market economy forced the people of China, accustomed to little personal choice, to accept a frightening amount of uncertainty and responsibility for making their own lives work.

Deng Xiaoping and the pragmatists had anticipated that many would suffer in the transition. But they had calculated correctly that the vast majority of Chinese would welcome the new level of personal responsibility. The guarantees and security of the old system were gone, but the freedom and possibilities of the new system inspired a tremendous outpouring of economic creativity and effort.

By the time Deng Xiaoping died in 1997, China was in the midst of an unparalleled economic boom and was well on the way to becoming a superpower. The less fortunate—tens of millions of them—still lived in poverty, their lives desperately short of such basics as electricity and clean water. Yet the overall level of prosperity in China had reached levels unimaginable when Mao died in 1976. Hard and difficult as the transition was, the great majority of Chinese took pride in the improving economic conditions in China.

The world had realized that the introduction of the socialist market economy was a decisive and probably permanent shift in direction for China. Foreign investment poured in, rising from $11 billion in 1992 to $42.1 billion by 2000.

The pragmatists were firmly in control of the government and the party at the turn of the millennium. The debate between the pragmatic backers of Deng Xiaoping's vision of a socialist market economy and the hard-liners favoring central planning and the retention of crucial parts of the Maoist vision had largely ceased. Li Peng stepped down as premier in 1998 after his constitutionally allotted two terms in office, his place taken by Zhu Rongji. That Li Peng retired gracefully was itself a major event. The leaders of the previous generation had held onto power, either formally or informally, with little or no constitutional restraint. But the adoption of a Western-style constitution providing for fixed terms greatly reduced the risk of another "cult of personality" and dictatorial rule by a single man or woman. Despite the continued dominance of the political process by the CCP, China was becoming increasingly a country of laws, not men.

Local elections were instituted at the township level late in the decade. On the provincial and national levels the people's congresses, once mere rubberstamps for the decisions of the Party, assumed a larger part in making policy. Democratic reformers in and out of China had hoped for more rapid progress in the wake of the collapse of Soviet communism. But in China the CCP remained firmly in control. Although many, perhaps a majority of Chinese still favored democratic reform, a survey of attitudes conducted in 1997 showed that most Chinese were satisfied with a gradual evolution of democratic institutions under the leadership of the CCP while the nation concentrated on economic progress. John Gittings in his book *The Changing Face of China* quotes one young businessman: "We are prepared to let these old fellows take their time. The main thing is that they should go smoothly.... In ten year's time, that's when we expect to see real change."

Traffic, Beijing

Chapter 11
China and the World

The world watched China's development in the 1990's with a mixture of anticipation and concern. China's market of well over a billion potential consumers held great promise for increased trade and economic growth for China's neighbors and trading nations around the world. A China participating in international organizations was certainly far preferable to its belligerent isolation of the past. China's participation in efforts to preserve peace, protect the global environment, and raise living standards in poor nations would be welcomed by all.

On the other hand, the sheer immensity of China's resources and potential power created deep concern in foreign capitals. China's inexpensive products and huge pool of cheap labor might devastate the economies of other nations and upset efforts to promote free trade. A prosperous China could build a formidable modern army, becoming a regional and even a global bully. China's drive to modernize at all costs might cause industrial pollution that would poison the water and air far beyond its borders.

DIPLOMATIC OFFENSIVE

The pragmatic leaders of the PRC recognized that China needed to allay the world's concerns. They started a vigorous diplomatic offensive to convince other nations that China's development could benefit all nations. China should not be viewed as an economic competitor, they argued, but as great investment, an economic partner, and a force for peace.

Chinese diplomacy took a realistic, non-ideological line. China was no longer interested in exporting communism but in doing business. China's leaders sought investment aggressively, altering policies to make conditions more attractive to international banks and corporations. In exchange for formal trade and diplomatic ties, the PRC required other nations to first drop their diplomatic recognition of the Nationalist Republic of China on Taiwan. By 2007, only 23 nations maintained full diplomatic relations with Taiwan while 161 recognized the PRC.

Five American presidents whose policies involved the PRC.
At the dedication of the Ronald Reagan Presidential Library:
George H. Bush, Reagan, Jimmy Carter, Gerald Ford, and Richard Nixon.

HEALING WOUNDS, MAKING FRIENDS

China moved to repair quarrels with several of its neighbors. Decades of distrust between China and the former Soviet Union had led to a heavy military buildup along shared borders and armed clashes in 1969. In the summer of 2001, President Jiang Zemin met with Russian Federation President Vladimir Putin (1952–   ) to sign a Treaty of Friendship and Cooperation. Putin and Jiang joined with the leaders of four Central Asian countries, Kazakhstan, Kyrgystan, Tajikistan, and Uzbekistan—all former member states of the Soviet Union—to found the Shanghai Cooperation Organization for promoting regional stability, fighting terrorism, and negotiating joint development projects. China began helping Kazakhstan to develop its oil fields, the two jointly building a long pipeline that would help secure oil-hungry China's energy supply. China invested large sums in hydroelectric projects in Kyrgystan and Tajikistan that would soon bring critically needed electricity into the immense undeveloped lands the three nations shared in Central Asia.

China and India, both developing powers with huge populations, had long been rivals. In 1962, the two had fought a brief war over disputed borderlands. Most of these disputes were finally resolved in talks in 2003, opening a new relationship. The two nations engaged in a booming trade and began planning joint military exercises. By 2008, Indian experts predicted that the PRC would be India's leading trading partner. China plowed aid and investment into neighboring Bangladesh, helping one of the world's poorest nations to raise its wretched standard of living.

China continued a special relationship with Pakistan through aid, investment, and regional security plans. Together the two nations began building a rail and pipeline link from China to the Persian Gulf, where the port of Gwader would soon become one of the world's most modern shipping terminals. One commentator likened the pipeline in importance to the Panama Canal in the Western Hemisphere. To insure future oil supplies, China also pursued friendly relations with Saudi Arabia and Iran. China's arms exports to Iran and help with Iran's nuclear program came as unwelcome developments for the United States.

The leaders of the PRC took a particular interest in Southeast Asia. China moved to resolve disputes with Vietnam. As recently as 1979, the two nations had come to blows over borders and Vietnamese military actions in Cambodia and Laos. Although still wary after centuries of antipathy, the two nations began forging peaceful links.

Vietnam is one of the ten members of the Association of Southeast Asian Nations (ASEAN), along with the Philippines, Indonesia, Malaysia, Singapore, Thailand, Brunei, Myanmar, Cambodia, and Laos. China began cooperating with ASEAN on trade relations, suggesting a trading bloc to compete with the United States and the European Union. In 1997, ASEAN instituted ASEAN Plus Three (China, Japan, and South Korea) conferences. In 2005, the ASEAN Plus Three nations invited Australia, New Zealand, and India to join in the first East Asia Summit. The potential of this emerging bloc of nations may considerably change the dynamics of the world's trade, security, and conflict resolution in the years to come.

China reached out to Africa and South America in search of new markets and friends. Particularly in Africa, where many authoritarian regimes continued in power, China's realistic, non-judgmental foreign policy built relationships that Western industrial nations refused. In some particularly poor countries, China extended modest aid packages. In the Caribbean, the PRC became one of Cuba's most important allies, enjoying much of the influence once exercised by the Soviet Union.

A TROUBLED RELATIONSHIP

China's relations with Japan presented particularly difficult problems. From the 1890's to the end of World War II in 1945, Japan followed a policy of stunning aggressiveness and brutality toward China. With aid from the

United States, Japan had emerged from defeat in World War II to become East Asia's largest economy—far too important a market and a source of investment for the PRC to ignore.

A stamp of the Yasukuni Shrine

While many average Chinese continued to nurse hatred for the Japanese, the pragmatic leaders of the PRC moved to improve relations. Japan and China made common cause against the expansion of Soviet influence in East Asia in the 1980's. Japanese investment and the importation of Japanese factory equipment were essential to China's economic development in the 1980's and 1990's. Recently, the two have participated in the six-party talks aimed at ending North Korea's nuclear weapons program. In 2004, China passed the United States to become Japan's largest trading partner.

Yet the Sino-Japanese relationship remains troubled. Both nations claim the Senkaku Islands. Japan has increased the budget and reach of its "self-defense forces" with the encouragement of the United States. In the summer of 2007, it launched a helicopter carrier, Japan's largest warship since World War II. Some analysts predicted that Japan was planning to build a full-sized aircraft carrier in the near future. Equipped with the American Aegis radar system, Japan's warships are already among the world's most advanced.

China complained strenuously when Japanese prime ministers visited the Yasukuni Shrine where fourteen war criminals were buried along with common soldiers. Further complaints came when new Japanese textbooks downplayed Japanese atrocities in China during World War II, particularly the Rape of Nanjing. Although Japanese Prime Minister Tomiichi Murayama (1924–) apologized in 1995 for Japan's wartime aggression—an apology repeated by subsequent prime ministers—many Chinese doubted Japan's sincerity. As recently as 2005, widespread and violent protests over the disputed islands and Japan's "insufficient" apologies have erupted in China. Practical matters of trade and investment remain too important for either nation to curtail, but Japan remains deeply unpopular with the Chinese people.

THE OTHER CHINA

The future of Taiwan remains by far the largest issue in China's relationship with the international community. The issue is so delicate and so complex that small shades in the meaning of words take on great significance for leaders on both sides of the Taiwan Strait. Leaders of the PRC dislike the term "China-Taiwan relationship" because it seems to imply that they are separate and independent nations. The PRC maintains that Taiwan is a rogue province and that its future is a domestic matter, not subject to the interference of other nations. The diplomatically correct phrase is "cross-Strait relationship."

Taiwanese leaders counter that the island was not a part of a united ancient China. Previously called Formosa, the island did not come under the rule of China until conquered by the Qing Dynasty in 1683. Most of Taiwan's people today descend from early Han immigrants who intermarried with the original aboriginal inhabitants. Over the centuries, the descendents of these unions began thinking of themselves as "native Taiwanese." Resenting the control of the distant imperial government, the majority of Taiwanese longed for independence.

Japan took possession of Taiwan following the Sino-Japanese War of 1895, instituting brutal rule over the Taiwanese. To the bitter disappointment of the islanders, the Allies turned Taiwan over to the Nationalist forces of Chiang Kai-shek after the defeat of Japan in 1945. Trouble soon followed. On February 28, 1947, Nationalist officials beat an old woman selling black market cigarettes and shot a passerby who tried to intervene. The Taiwanese rose in outrage. On March 8, Nationalist troops attacked the rioters, killing an estimated 20,000. Nationalist authorities clamped marshal law on Taiwan. It would not be lifted until 1985. In December 1947, Communist forces drove the Nationalists off the Mainland. Chiang and what was left of his army withdrew to Taiwan. Eventually refugees from the Mainland would number about 12% of the population.

Taipei

Chiang claimed that the Nationalist Republic of China (ROC) was the legitimate government of China and that its army would one day return to conquer the Mainland. In reality, Chiang lacked the equipment and manpower. Even the existence of the ROC depended on the protection of the United States, particularly its powerful Seventh Fleet. On June 27, 1950, two days after the outbreak of war in Korea, President Harry S Truman officially promised that the United States would come to the aid of Taiwan in case of an attack. By the end of 1951, the United States was pouring military and economic aid into the island.

Taiwan prospered with the aid and protection of the United States. Most nations followed the lead of the United States in continuing to recognize the ROC as the rightful government of China. By the late 1960's, Taiwan was a huge economic success. However, its uncertain status made it vulnerable to the power politics of great nations. In February 1972, President Nixon made his historic visit to China, signaling that the United States would concentrate on improving relations with the PRC while dealing with Taiwan as an inconvenient afterthought. A bitter Taiwan was ejected from the U.N., its seats in the General Assembly and on the Security Council awarded to the PRC. More humiliation followed as nations scrambled to shift diplomatic recognition from the ROC to the PRC.

Chiang Kai-shek died on April 5, 1975. He was succeeded by his cautiously liberal son, Chiang Ching-kuo (1910–1988), who gradually opened the political process on Taiwan. This new direction troubled the leaders of the PRC. Since the revolution, the ROC had been a one-party state. Somewhat ironically, the leaders of the PRC preferred dealing with their old enemies in the Nationalist party to the possibility of having to convince a democratically elected government that the PRC could be trusted.

On December 15, 1978, the United States terminated diplomatic relations with Taiwan, turning over responsibility to an officially private agency, the American Institute in Taiwan. (American diplomats "on leave" staff the institute.) The commitment of the United States to protect Taiwan continued unchanged.

"ONE CHINA, TWO SYSTEMS"

In 1981, the PRC offered an eleven-point plan to the Nationalists. If the Nationalists agreed to the reunification of Taiwan and the Mainland, the PRC would allow Taiwan to keep its independent economic system, laws, and even its own defense force. Chiang Ching-kuo refused to negotiate a "one China, two systems" approach until the informal relationship between the two Chinas improved. The PRC accepted his stance and the animosity between the two Chinas eased in the 1980's. Indirect trade and investment boomed. For the first time, the PRC allowed Chinese who had fled to Taiwan during the revolution to visit their families on the Mainland. Sports teams exchanged visits. Officials met informally at regional conferences to discuss improving relations.

Chiang Ching-kuo allowed native Taiwanese participation in the government for the first time. He named a native Taiwanese vice president in 1984, a move the leaders of the PRC feared might indicate a declining belief that China could ever be reunified under any system. In 1985, Chiang Ching-kuo lifted martial law. Newspapers and opponents of the government began cautiously discussing the shape of Taiwan's future.

Lee Teng-hui

Chiang Ching-kuo died in 1988, his place as president taken by the native Taiwanese Lee Teng-hui. A year later, the brutal suppression of the Tiananmen Square demonstrations soured the improving mood between the two Chinas. Lee speeded up democratic reforms. He allowed the formation of opposition political parties, among them the pro-independence Democratic Progressive Party.

"A NEW WORLD ORDER"

The collapse of the Soviet Union in 1991 removed a major reason for the United States to push for better relations with the PRC. Nixon and Kissinger had seen China as a counterbalance to the Soviet Union in the competition between the two superpowers. But without the Soviet threat, the "strategic relationship" with the PRC declined in importance. President William J. Clinton (president from 1993–2001) tilted American policy toward furthering human rights in China. The Chinese found America's emphasis on civil rights hypocritical. They pointed to racism in the United States and particularly to the violent crime rate among the poor, neither of which were significant problems in the PRC.

Since the 1980's, China had been seeking membership in the World Trade Organization (WTO). China also wanted to host the 2000 Olympics, which would give it an opportunity to show off all that had been accomplished under reform. But it could achieve neither goal without the backing of the United States. The games went to Sydney, Australia, and the United States continued to insist that the PRC liberalize trade rules and civil rights before joining the WTO.

Taiwan scheduled its first direct presidential election for 1996. Horrified that the Taiwanese might elect the candidate of the Democratic Progressive Party, the PRC began another round of its periodic saber rattling. The United States responded by dispatching two carrier battle groups to Taiwanese waters in the largest deployment of its military since the end of the Vietnam War. In the tense atmosphere, Lee Teng-hui won reelection. The continuation of Nationalist rule eased the PRC's fears somewhat, and the armed forces of the PRC, Taiwan, and the United States stepped back from confrontation. However, Lee increasingly referred to Taiwan as a nation. Although he claimed to be looking forward to reunification with the Mainland, he promised the voters that no union would take place until the PRC became as democratic as Taiwan.

THE RETURN OF HONG KONG

Hong Kong provided an opportunity for the PRC to demonstrate the "one China, two systems" plan it had proposed for Taiwan. Great Britain had gained control of the island of Hong Kong and the area surrounding its magnificent harbor in the Opium Wars (1840–1843 and 1856–1860). In 1898, Britain negotiated the use of additional territory in exchange for a ninety-nine-year lease. Under British rule, the Crown Colony of Hong Kong became one of the world's great trading ports: "the Pearl of the Orient."

Both sides offered concessions when negotiations opened in the early 1980's on the future of Hong Kong. The Chinese were anxious to erase the vestige of Western imperialism in China. At the same time, they saw the advantage of preserving Hong Kong as a trading center and a source of hard currency. The British wanted to avoid the expense of protecting Hong Kong while also preserving the profitable business conducted by scores of its companies in the colony.

In 1984, the two nations issued a joint declaration that Britain would surrender control of Hong Kong in 1997. In exchange, the PRC would allow Hong Kong to retain its independent economic system, laws, and a certain amount of self-government for at least fifty years. On July 1, 1997, Hong

Kong became a "special administrative region" of the PRC. On December 20, 1999, Portugal gave up rights to its colony of Macao, 37 miles (60 km.) southwest of Hong Kong.

Hong Kong

A shipping company owner, Tung Chee-hwa, became Hong Kong's first chief executive with the backing of the Party Central Committee of the PRC. By 1999, the Central Committee was pressuring Tung to restrict civil rights in Hong Kong. In 2003, a seemingly innocuous change sparked widespread protests in Hong Kong. The Central Committee backed down, and Tung resigned not long after. However, skeptics in Taiwan and elsewhere became more suspicious of the PRC's "one China, two systems" approach to reunification of Taiwan and the Mainland. Recognizing its mistake, the PRC largely kept hands off Hong Kong in the next few years. In 2007, the people of Hong Kong enthusiastically celebrated the tenth anniversary of "the return to the motherland."

"THE BILL AND JIANG SHOW"
Following the 1996 military confrontation over Taiwan's free elections, the leaders of the United States and the PRC reevaluated the risk of

miscalculation or accident triggering war. President Clinton exerted his great personal charm to warm relations. President Jiang Zemin made a successful visit to the United States in the fall of 1997, and Clinton paid a return visit to China the following summer. So famously did the two leaders get on that reporters started to refer to them as "the Bill and Jiang show," ignoring the fact that Jiang was the Chinese president's surname, not his given name, Zemin.

Clinton and Jiang discussed several crucial issues. Jiang wanted the United States to discourage Taiwan's growing independence movement and to help China gain admission to the WTO. In return, Clinton asked better access for American businesses to China's market and urged more liberal civil rights. Both sides agreed to renew the "strategic relationship" in the interests of preserving peace.

Negotiations were nearly complete for China's entry into the WTO in March 1999 as Premier Zhu Rongji landed in the United States for what he expected would be a triumphal visit. But the visit turned into a disaster. Advisors to Clinton urged him to press the Chinese for last-minute concessions protecting the American clothing industry. China, with its immense pool of low-cost labor, could drive American manufacturers out of business unless China controlled the volume and cost of its clothing exports. The issue was complicated by a major civil rights issue: the right of Chinese workers to form independent trade unions. Labor negotiations would raise workers' pay and bring China's exports more in line with global prices. But the Chinese leadership firmly opposed independent trade unions, fearing the political power such unions would accumulate and the impact of higher labor costs on China's trade balance. A two-hour meeting between Zhu and Clinton failed to break the impasse, once again thwarting China's entry into the WTO.

The disappointment was a major loss of face for Zhu, Jiang, and their fellow pragmatists. The hard-liners took the opportunity to criticize the leadership, likening the United States' bargaining position to Japan's extortionate Twenty-one Demands of 1915. Not since Tiananmen Square had a single issue so dominated public discussion in the PRC. America had once seemed a beacon of hope and freedom, but now it seemed just a self-interested bully intent on wringing a last concession from the weaker member of the "strategic relationship."

THE BOMBING OF THE BELGRADE EMBASSY

The grumbling would soon escalate into angry anti-American demonstrations. Since 1995 the North Atlantic Treaty Organization (NATO) had periodically used air strikes to separate warring factions in splintering Yugoslavia. In 1999, NATO launched a new campaign to force the withdrawal of Christian Serbian forces from the breakaway Muslim province of Kosovo. On May 7, American aircraft accidentally bombed the Chinese embassy in Belgrade, killing three Chinese journalists.

The Chinese responded angrily. The government demanded an apology while crowds demonstrated in front of Western embassies in Beijing. Numerous allegations, never proven, were made in China and the West that the bombing had been intentional. The government of the United States apologized and agreed to pay the families of the dead, but the Chinese were slow to forgive.

The tension with the United States contributed to a new nationalism in the PRC. A hastily written book, *China Can Say No*, became a bestseller with the message that China should take a firm line with the West, demanding recognition as a great power economically, politically, and militarily. Other books and articles with similar messages gained wide readership, particularly among young intellectuals.

Faced with the rising power of hard-line sentiments in the PRC, Jiang demonstrated great political skill. He reduced the power of the controversial Zhu Rongji and assumed some of the hard-liners' rhetoric in his statements within China. Outside of China, Jiang practiced careful diplomacy, hoping with mild words to win China's bid to host the 2008 Olympics and entry into the WTO. In July 2001, the International Olympic Committee accepted China's bid for the games. The outpouring of jubilation by China's masses boosted the popularity of Jiang's government. In November 2001, China was at last admitted to the WTO. Jiang's triumph marked the end of fifteen years of negotiations.

NO'S AND WITHOUT'S

During his visit to the PRC in the summer of 1998, President Clinton accepted the central government's "Three No's" policy: 1. No two Chinas; 2. No independence for Taiwan; and 3. No membership for Taiwan in international organizations accepting only independent countries as members. Shortly after Clinton left China, his staff issued a statement that Clinton's acceptance did not indicate a change in United States foreign policy. Yet the PRC was elated, Taiwan seriously worried.

On March 18, 2000, Taiwan held its second free presidential election, electing the pro-independence Chen Shui-bian of the Democratic Progressive Party. The United States, in the midst of its own presidential election, hardly seemed to notice, but the PRC issued a warning that "Taiwan independence, in whatever form, will never be allowed."

Chen calmed the situation when he laid out a response to the PRC's "Three No's" policy with his own "Four No's and One Without" during his inauguration speech on May 20, 2000: 1. Taiwan's government would not declare independence; 2. The Republic of China would not change its name to the Republic of Taiwan; 3. Taiwan would not add to its constitution the doctrine of "special state-to-state relations" (a concept declaring that Taiwan already functioned as an independent nation in its relationship with the PRC); and 4. That the government would not promote a referendum on unification or independence. The "without" pledged that Chen would not abolish the National Unification Council, a powerless agency founded in 1990 but whose continued existence had symbolic value.

The "Four No's and One Without" was a disappointment to those Taiwanese who favored immediate independence, but it satisfied the PRC and the United States. In the following years, leaders of both nations would repeatedly demand assurances from Taiwan that the policy remained in effect.

President Jiang Zemin,
President George W. Bush, and their wives

A NEW AMERICAN ADMINISTRATION

In January 2001, George W. Bush (1946–   ) became president of the United States. Under the influence of hard-line "neo-conservatives," Bush stated that he considered America's relationship with the PRC more one of competition than cooperation. The "strategic relationship" was further undercut by Bush's commitment to the National Missile Defense System, which the United States planned to share with Japan and perhaps Taiwan.

In April 2001, a Chinese fighter collided with an American spy plane off the southern coast of China. The Chinese pilot was killed and the American plane was forced to make an emergency landing on the island of Hainan, where its crew was held for ten days. Once again Chinese young people took to the streets in anti-American demonstrations. Ignoring an already tense situation, Bush approved the largest arms sale to Taiwan in a decade. China's ambassador warned that the relationship of the two nations was "at a crossroads."

The neo-conservatives within the Bush administration preached that the PRC had become America's principal strategic rival and potential military antagonist. Although military analysts outside the administration pointed out that Chinese defense expenditures were only a small fraction of the United States military budget, the view persisted within the administration.

TERRORISTS STRIKE

On September 11, 2001, two airliners hijacked by Arab terrorists crashed into the World Trade Center in New York City. Bush launched a worldwide campaign against terrorism. Heeding the advice of Secretary of State Colin Powell (1937–), Bush sought the help of the PRC while visiting Shanghai for a meeting of the Asia Pacific Economic Conference in October. The Chinese were quick to signal their willingness to cooperate in "the war on terror," particularly against the radical Islamic Taliban in Afghanistan, a regime the Chinese feared might have a dangerous influence among Muslims in the PRC's far western Xinjiang Province.

While most of the world focused on the Mideast, Taiwan held legislative on December 1, 2001. For the first time, a majority of seats went to the pro-independence Democratic Progressive Party. Again the PRC made a stern statement warning against a move toward independence.

The PRC protested the invasion of Iraq in the spring of 2002, favoring continued U.N. weapons inspections. It did send some humanitarian aid during the occupation of Iraq and agreed to cancel Iraqi debt. Nearly a dozen Chinese aid workers were killed trying to assist in the war-torn country.

PULLING THE DRAGON'S TAIL

In December 2003, at a time when the United States was concentrating its military and diplomatic efforts on the Mideast, Taiwan's president, Chen

Shui-bian, scheduled a national referendum for March 20, 2004, nine days before the presidential election. To outsiders, the referendum seemed harmless, calling only for the PRC to remove the hundreds of missiles aimed at the island and to renounce force in further dealings with Taiwan. Yet in the subtle world of Chinese politics, the leaders of the PRC saw the vote as a referendum on Taiwanese independence since it seemed to imply that Taiwan was already a country that could demand action by another country.

Anxious to maintain peace in East Asia while it was waging war in Iraq and Afghanistan, the United States demanded that Chen tone down the referendum. Although huffily asserting Taiwan's right to vote on any referendum its legislature proposed, Chen complied. The legislators sent two referendums to the voters. The first asked if Taiwan should increase defense spending if the PRC did not withdraw the missiles. The second asked if Taiwan should open negotiations with the PRC. Since the two referendums asked voters to express their opinion on what the Taiwanese government should do, not on what the government of the PRC should do, the wording was considered less diplomatically offensive. Still unhappy but somewhat mollified, the PRC toned down its threats.

The ignominious flap over the referendum demonstrated once again that Taiwan, for all its economic progress, remained critically dependent on the United States for its very existence. In March 2004, 80% of Taiwan's voters went to the polls, reelecting Chen by a narrow margin. Only 45% chose to vote for or against the referendums, too few to make the results binding.

In his inauguration speech for a second term, Chen made reference to but did not repeat the "Four No's and One Without" policy, an omission not lost on diplomats worried about another armed confrontation between the PRC on one side and Taiwan and the United States on the other. When Chen seemed to waffle on the policy in the months after, the 10th National People's Congress passed the Anti-Secession Law on March 14, 2005, threatening the use of "non-peaceful means" in response to a declaration of independence by Taiwan.

The Oriental Pearl radio tower, Shanghai

Chapter 12
China's Century?

The rapid emergence of a modern and confident China is an event so momentous as to be without precedent in world history. At the time of Mao's death in 1976, China was an impoverished third-world country. Today, China leads the world in the manufacture of consumer goods. It ranks third in factory output, first in agricultural production, and third in trade. In 2006, it surpassed Japan as the world's second largest producer of motor vehicles. Overall, it has the world's fourth largest economy.

Mao's commune system strangled the creativity and energy of the Chinese people. Its replacement by Deng Xiaoping's socialist market economy lifted 350 million people out of extreme poverty and released a flood of entrepreneurial activity.

Mao's Great Cultural Revolution went so badly awry in the decade before his death that China nearly dissolved into chaos. Today China has a stable if sometimes repressive government and an evolving legal system.

A nation with few friends and fewer admirers during the Maoist era, China is today a major force in international forums, its "soft diplomacy" exerting influence throughout Asia and beyond. With the reputation and example of the United States badly tarnished by American actions in the Middle East, many nations look to China for leadership in the evolution of peaceful co-existence among nations.

A visitor to the 2008 Olympics can be forgiven for concluding from the immense activity and progress evident around him that China's future is bright and that the 21st century may indeed prove to be "China's century." The reality is more complicated. For all the successes of reform in China, huge challenges lie ahead. China's status as a superpower is precarious. A reversal of the progress made since the pragmatists took charge in 1978 could throw the world into economic chaos and threaten peace and stability far beyond China's borders.

This may or may not be China's century, but what happens in China in the next decade or two may well determine the future of the world in our time. Although no one can predict with any certainty the shape of the future, we can at least examine a few of the critical issues facing China and what affect their outcome may have on the world.

**Mao and his times are
fading memories in today's China.**

THE STABILITY OF THE GOVERNMENT

Since the Tiananmen Square demonstrations in 1989, continued rule by the Chinese Communist Party has been based on an unwritten understanding between the Party and the people. The government under the control of the CCP will provide prosperity in exchange for the power to repress political movements—particularly democracy—and civil rights seen as threatening the stability of the regime. The understanding is not without challenges both internal and external. In private, a large number of Chinese express a longing for a true multiparty state with universal suffrage. The United States and other democratic nations continue to pressure the PRC to liberalize civil rights. Yet the majority of the Chinese people, at least for now, seem content to let the CCP remain in power so long as China's economic development continues at a rapid pace.

Scene of bitter fighting between soldiers and workers in 1989, Changan Boulevard is only another busy avenue in modern Beijing.

The leaders of the CCP have taken steps to legitimize the rule of the Party. Beginning with the diminution of Mao's cult of personality by Deng Xiaoping, the Party has worked to ensure that no single person will ever wield such power again. The constitution has been revised to resemble more closely those of the western democracies. The regular and nonviolent change in leadership has been one of the most important results of this adherence to constitutional requirements. In 2003, Jiang Zemin and Zhu Rongji left office after their mandated terms and were replaced by Hu Jintao (1942–   ) as president and Wen Jiabao (1942–) as premier.

Hu Jintao

The CCP has codified laws and developed the legal system, making China a nation of laws rather than powerful men. The accessibility of common folk to the courts in formal proceedings has added immensely to the perception that those accused of wrongdoing or seeking justice in a serious civil matter can expect verdicts according to the law rather than at the whim of Red Guards or Party bureaucrats. The courts handle few civil disputes since about 90% are resolved by the 980,000 mediation committees made up of informed citizens, a traditional way of resolving conflict in China that predates the revolution by millennia. Formalized by the CCP after the revolution, these committees were radicalized and given expanded powers as "people's courts." Restored to their traditional function under reform, they work well with only the rare civil dispute being appealed to the regular courts.

Hu Jintao and Wen Jiabao are the first president and premier to grow to adulthood since the revolution, giving rise to hopes that they may be more democratic than the leaders of the past. Ready access to the courts has been accompanied by limited democracy at the village and township levels. As the populace gains experience with the legal system and the electoral process, the people will become more assertive in their use, putting additional pressure on the CCP to liberalize civil rights.

The press has become more daring in discussing problems. The leaders, in turn, are more honest in responding. However, the government has resisted opening the flow of electronic information, spending heavily on Internet policing.

Freedom of assembly is still curtailed. Only government sanctioned unions and civic organizations are permitted. Participants in unauthorized public demonstrations risk retaliation. In December 2005, reports reached the West that twenty demonstrators in Dongzhou had been shot by police during a protest over the construction of a power plant. Undeterred, demonstrators still take to the streets in surprising numbers. The decade between 1995 and 2005 saw an increase in local protests from 10,000 to 75,000, according to the government's own reports. Faced with this trend, the government is being pushed to negotiate more and use repressive tactics less. Eventually, independent labor unions may become necessary to preserve domestic peace.

**A sign of the times: a Beijing subway
train passes advertisements for McDonald's.**

The success of the economy under reform has improved the lives of the vast majority of Chinese. However, the benefits are not equally distributed. Coastal provinces, workers outside of heavy industry, and the vast army of CCP bureaucrats benefit the most, inland provinces, industrial workers, and most agricultural workers the least. Poor housing, the decline in the quality of government services, and pollution brought on by rapid industrial development have a disproportionate affect on the less fortunate. In July 2007, Premier Wen Jiabao announced a new national health care plan to address the decline in health services.

Disparities in economic well-being threaten the return of the class divisions that eventually tore the old China apart and led to some forty years of violent upheaval. While maintaining the free market and the success of economic reform, the government must equalize the benefits through taxation and careful allocation of resources or risk the possible disruption of the socialist market economy by class hatred and violence.

The Chinese military possesses such overwhelming force that it is unlikely that independence movements in Tibet, Xinjiang, or elsewhere can successfully challenge the rule of the CCP. However, the recent history of Europe, the Middle East, and the United States has demonstrated the ability of a few violent extremists to disrupt societies. The Chinese government reports that Muslim revolutionaries in Xinjiang have sought and received help from international terrorist networks.

Provincial governors and military commanders have exercised considerable power in China for centuries. Even in the Maoist era, they often resisted direction by the central government. It is unlikely that any of these powerful officials will risk open rebellion. There is the risk, however, that prosperous provinces may refuse to abide by national policies that threaten their own prosperity for the benefit of less successful provinces. Often the central government has difficulty collecting all the taxes owed by provinces, some large corporations, and the very rich.

As part of the modernization program, China's military is better equipped and trained than ever before. Since the revolution, the army has been consistently—and often surprisingly—amenable to the leadership of the CCP. The Lin Biao plot, the only significant attempt since the revolution to manipulate the army's power, failed because of the loyalty of senior military officials. Army leaders have largely favored reform, but there remains a deeply conservative streak in their thinking. If they perceive that the reformers are going too far or if unrest threatens national stability, the army may cast aside its traditional subservience to the Party in favor of direct action and military rule.

Corruption, paternalism, patronage, and the emergence of a new, albeit small, class of the very wealthy could undermine the Party and the government. In 2007, China suffered a public relations disaster when tainted pet food killed dogs and cats in the United States. Investigations by the media revealed other tainted exports, including cough syrup, thought responsible for the death of ninety people in Panama. Zheng Xiaoyu, head of the State Food and Drug Administration, was tried, convicted, and executed for accepting bribes to approve untested products for export.

Only weeks later, American toy companies recalled millions of Chinese-manufactured toys because of lead paint and choking hazards. One Chinese factory owner killed himself. As this book goes to press, the Chinese government is trying desperately to implement effective testing and regulation to reassure trading partners that China's exports will be safer in the future. Foreign companies doing business in the PRC will need to cooperate with the government's effort. All too often foreign companies have been willing partners in bribery and avoiding regulations. Until foreign companies and the governments of their home countries improve business ethics, problems with safety seem likely to continue.

UNCONTROLLABLE FORCES?

For all the problems unresolved or created by reform, the overwhelming evidence demonstrates the huge and far-reaching success of the pragmatic policies initiated by Deng Xiaoping and ably executed by his successors. But reform has unleashed forces that may be beyond any government to control

Among history's lessons two in particular seem to put in doubt the ability of the CCP to maintain its current position. The overturning of regimes and sometimes entire governmental systems usually occurs not when the population is ground down and largely destitute of hope but in times of rising expectations. So it was in 1911 when the Nationalist Revolution overthrew the rule of the emperors. Today, the expectations of the Chinese people are much higher and—if history is a guide—the rule of the Party is similarly at risk if it fails to introduce democratic reforms to match the progress in the economy.

Likewise, a prosperous and expanding middle class usually provides the political leadership of revolutionary movements. Virtually nonexistent a generation ago, China's entrepreneurial middle class is today a dynamic and growing segment of society. Deng Xiaoping recognized the need for a middle class to lead and provide the example for economic reform. Today, that same middle class is increasingly unhappy with its lack of political power. The Democracy Movement may be quiescent in China now, but it seems certain to recover a voice eventually, as it did in 1911, 1919, 1957, 1978, and 1989. The next time the combination of the passion of the students and intellectuals and the economic resources and pragmatism of the middle class may combine to pose an even greater threat to the regime than presented by the Tiananmen demonstrations of 1989.

**Shanghai's Maglev train runs from the airport
to downtown at a speed of 267 miles/hour (433 km/h).**

CONTINUED ECONOMIC GROWTH

Economic growth at the current rate of 9% may become difficult for China to maintain. China has been fortunate in the era of reform, but inflation, business conditions elsewhere in the world, regional or internal unrest, the availability of critical resources, natural disaster, international relations—particularly with the United States—and a host of other factors could cause a downturn in the economy.

China graduates more students with business degrees than any other country in the world, but there is still a lack of skilled management, particularly in state-owned enterprises. (According to a recent survey, only 20% of factory managers had business degrees.) Despite the shift to the socialist market economy, Party and government bureaucracies have grown under reform, creating additional layers of redundancy and lowering productivity.

The government still runs some 25,000 state-owned enterprises, most in heavy industry and utilities. Many factories are badly out of date, their workers frustrated by low or late payment of wages, and their managers overwhelmed by the complexities of competing in the global market. The state-owned enterprises continue to drain huge sums from the government treasury.

Agricultural incomes lag. The local manufacturing enterprises have not grown fast enough or competed successfully enough to absorb the excess labor in the countryside. In 2006, the government cancelled the agriculture tax, reducing the farmers' overall tax burden and providing a boost to incomes and rural employment. However, the gap between urban and rural incomes remains among the world's largest.

Inadequate transportation increases the cost of both agricultural and manufactured products produced in the interior provinces. Despite massive investment in infrastructure, China still lacks enough modern highways, efficient waterways, airports, power plants, and sewage disposal facilities. It will take years, probably decades, before China can boast an infrastructure on a par with that of Japan, the United States, and the European countries. Modernizing China's infrastructure will require immense sums, challenging the ability of the government and heavily taxed private enterprises to meet workers' demands for better living standards.

The cost of transportation and chemical fertilizers help drive high inflation in the cost of food. The price of foodstuffs was rising at 18.2% as of the fall of 2007, outstripping a 6.5% increase in household incomes at a time when Chinese families were already spending 37% of their income on food. (American families spend 14%.)

Wage inequalities, the length of the workweek, and working conditions are the principal concerns of workers in all industries. The government treads a thin line between rewarding workers adequately and maintaining the competitive advantage of Chinese products in international trade. Eventually, whatever the impact on the trade balance and economic growth, the government will have to increase worker compensation and improve conditions or risk an unacceptable increase in strikes and other work actions. The formation of free labor unions would give Chinese workers the opportunity to negotiate better wages, a shorter workweek, and safer and healthier conditions. But the CCP remains opposed, insisting that workers are adequately represented by the largely powerless All China Federation of Trade Unions sanctioned by the Party.

In June 2007, the Standing Committee of the People's Congress passed a labor law that should correct some employer abuses, particularly the nonpayment of wages and the poor treatment of migrant workers. However, labor activists see the law as still too friendly to large companies, including foreign corporations doing business in China.

China's workforce is aging. Awash in excess labor today, Chinese industry may suffer from chronic labor shortages in twenty years.

**Many grandparents take care of
grandchildren while parents work.**

FOREIGN TRADE

The growth of China's economy has been largely based on foreign investment, exports, and a large trade balance. China continues to attract foreign investment on a massive scale—an estimated $70 billion in 2007. However, investing in China or doing business directly with the Chinese is neither easy nor necessarily profitable.

Since joining the World Trade Organization, the Chinese government has reduced tariffs and worked to ease the difficulties encountered by foreign companies in China. However, regulations, taxes, and laws are often confusing and their enforcement inconsistent. Appeal to the courts or regulatory agencies can be frustrating and time-consuming. Corruption and the expectation of bribes and kickbacks by bureaucrats complicate negotiations and threaten business ethics. Although energetic, Chinese workers often lack elementary skills. Government policies continue to restrict consumer spending. Taken altogether, these problems make it more difficult for foreign companies to earn acceptable returns on investment.

Foreign companies also have difficulty protecting intellectual property rights. For decades the PRC refused to sign the International Copyright Convention. It is now a signatory, but the piracy of CDs, DVDs, books, and computer programs is still a major problem.

Confronted with massive trade deficits, the United States and other nations have urged the government of the PRC to stimulate consumer spending. So far, however, Chinese policies have been focused on increasing sales abroad. The advantage that Chinese exports have is directly related to the exchange rate of China's monetary unit, the rimimbi, which is some 40% undervalued by 2007 estimates. An increase in the rimimbi's value would increase consumer spending, import sales, and the profitability of foreign companies while decreasing the deficits of China's trading partners.

The PRC's failure to move in the direction of a more equitable trading relationship with its partners has brought accusations that China is pursuing a mercantile policy overly favorable to its own economic development at the expense of trading partners, the future of the free trade system, and the health of the international economy. For the present, it appears that foreign companies find investment in China too tempting to pull back. Consumers in America and around the world enjoy the cheap prices of Chinese products. However, China's massive trade surpluses cannot continue indefinitely without risking the imposition of high tariffs and other trade restrictions damaging to all parties.

Vietnam, India, Indonesia, Pakistan, Bangladesh, and Russia are increasingly attractive to foreign businesses looking for cheap sources of labor and attractive business climates. A significant shift of investment away from China would bring downward pressure on China's economic growth.

INTERNATIONAL RELATIONS

China is increasingly the dominant nation in Asia, its economic progress envied and its political power acknowledged. The socialist market economy, where a single party makes the rules with the acquiescence of the population, has become a tempting model for other authoritarian regimes, particularly in poor countries.

The United States has seen its reputation seriously damaged by its occupation of Iraq. The Bush administration's "neo-con" foreign policy is interpreted by Asians as bullying and a quest for domination. Equally disturbing to many Asian governments is the inconsistency of American foreign policy which may change in favor of a Democratic, pro-human rights stance once the Bush administration leaves office, only to swing back to the neo-conservative perspective in four or eight years.

Neo-cons within the Bush administration have painted China as an emerging military threat to the United States. With American forces stretched thin by the Iraq war, there are some grounds for these concerns. China has made considerable progress in modernizing its military and developing military applications of space and computer technologies. But in its long history China has never been an aggressive military power, and its defense budget remains only about a tenth of what the United States spends. Unless confronted with American military adventurism in Asia, it is unlikely that China will change its defensive posture.

The "soft diplomacy" of the PRC has won friends in Asia and beyond. A major trading bloc is emerging through the ASEAN Plus Three mechanism. It appears that the PRC is working toward recruiting many of the same nations into a regional defense alliance. Pakistan, an ally of the United States, has even closer ties with the PRC. Should Pakistan decide that its interests no longer coincide with those of the United States, America could lose a critical ally in the Middle East.

In August 2005, Russia and the PRC held joint military maneuvers in Shandong Province. In August 2007, Russia, China, and the other members of the Shanghai Cooperation Organization held maneuvers on Russian soil. During the exercises, Premier Putin announced that Russia was resuming long-range patrols by its strategic bombers, the first time this force has been deployed since the breakup of the Soviet Union. The patrols represent a further hardening of Russia's stance toward the United States. If Russia and the PRC resume the alliance that the Soviet Union once had with the PRC, together they could pose a major threat to the United States in either a nuclear or conventional war. Even without armed conflict, the possibility of a new Cold War concerns many diplomats.

The joint maneuvers were aimed in part at the threat of a remilitarized Japan. The Bush administration has encouraged Japan to enlarge its military budget and to expand the reach of its "self-defense forces." During joint exercises with United States forces in the summer of 2007, Japanese pilots dropped live bombs for the first time since World War II—a step the Chinese saw as fraught with symbolism. Should Japan choose to increase its defense budget by a significant amount, China will react by spending more on its military, possibly leading to a dangerous arms race in East Asia.

Russia, the United States, China, and Japan have cooperated in the Six Party Talks with North and South Korea over the development of nuclear weapons by North Korea. In the summer of 2007, it appeared that North Korea was cutting back and perhaps ending its nuclear weapons program. Resumption will tax the patience of all the participants in the talks and possibly lead to threats of military action against North Korea by the United States or—possibly—the PRC.

The Donghai Bridge, the longest cross-sea bridge in the world (20.2 mi./32.5 km), connects Shanghai and the offshore port of Yangshan.

The general direction of China's foreign policy, including its relationship with the United States, has been toward peace. Its diplomats are as adept as any in the world at sounding harsh one moment, conciliatory the next. The Chinese are inclined to approach disputes with indirection, negotiating toward a solution that gives them an advantage but that does not crush adversaries, thus avoiding a lasting and dangerous bitterness on the part of the losers.

The PRC was the first nuclear power to renounce first use of nuclear weapons. In 1986, it renounced atmospheric testing. It agreed to the nuclear Non-Proliferation Treaty in 1992. Its representatives signed the Comprehensive Test Ban Treaty in 1996.

As well as the U.N., the WTO, ASEAN Plus Three, and the Shanghai Cooperation Organization, the PRC participates in a numerous other international organizations including the International Atomic Energy Agency (IAEA) and the World Health Organization (WHO). It maintains dozens of formal and informal exchanges of scientific information with other countries, including the United States–China Science and Technology Agreement.

**President Chen Shui-bian
of Taiwan**

TAIWANESE INDEPENDENCE?

The future of Taiwan remains one of the world's most dangerous issues. Hoping to maintain the status quo, the United States continues a policy of diplomatic ambiguity. A clear statement denying the PRC's claim to Taiwan could lead to diplomatic and trade retaliation by the PRC. A statement recognizing the claim would amount to acceptance of the PRC's contention that Taiwan is a rogue province and the "cross-Strait relationship" is a domestic matter that China's central government would be justified in resolving by military action. Caught between dangerous alternatives, the United States can do little but urge both sides to seek peaceful resolution of their differences while at the same time maintaining defense commitments to Taiwan and a major trade relationship with the PRC.

Pro-independence forces on Taiwan have become increasingly assertive. On March 4, 2007, President Chen Shui-bian announced a dramatic reversal of the "Four No's and One Without" policy, replacing it with the "Four Yeses and One No": 1. Taiwan wants independence; 2. Taiwan wants to change its formal name from The Republic of China to Taiwan or the Republic of Taiwan; 3. Taiwan wants a new constitution; and 4. Taiwan wants development. The "One No" (which might have been better left a "without") states that Taiwanese politics is without questions of left or right but only of unification or independence.

Both the PRC and the United States demanded that Taiwan's government return to the "Four No's and One Without" policy, but Chen pushed ahead. On July 19, 2007, Taiwan formally petitioned the United Nations for recognition as an independent country. The United Nations legal office returned Taiwan's application the next day, citing United Nations Resolution 2758 which declared in 1971 that the government of the PRC is the only legitimate representative of the Chinese people. President Chen's office responded: "Taiwan is a sovereign, independent country. Neither Taiwan nor China is subject to the other's jurisdiction. Moreover, Taiwan has never been part of China. This is the status quo."

On August 8, 2007, President Bush and President Hu Jintao reaffirmed their countries' commitment to United Nations Resolution 2758. Chen is scheduled to leave office in May 2008. It seems likely that he will seek referendums on a new constitution, on a change in Taiwan's formal name, and possibly on independence during the spring elections that will choose a new president. Only months before the PRC welcomes the world to the 2008 Olympics, a Taiwanese vote for independence could bring a superpower confrontation of potentially devastating consequences.

SUPERPOWER CONFRONTATION?

The options available to the leaders of the PRC and the United States are limited in the event of a Taiwanese vote for independence. The vast majority of the PRC's 1.3 billion people are fiercely dedicated to the unification of the Mainland and Taiwan. The power of the CCP is not invulnerable, and its leaders will have to take strong action to thwart Taiwanese independence or face an outcry from the Chinese people that would dwarf the Tiananmen protests of 1989.

Commitment to Taiwan is one of the "hot button" issues in American politics. A failure by the Bush administration to respond strongly to any action by the PRC would devastate the administration's popularity among conservatives and tear the Republican Party apart in an election year.

War between the superpowers is the worst scenario but not the only one. The PRC has some $1.3 trillion invested in the American economy, mostly in United States Treasury Bonds. A move to withdraw a massive amount would bankrupt the United States government and throw the American and world economies into depression. Or the United States could freeze the PRC's assets, bringing down the Chinese economy and probably the world economy as well.

The best hope is that careful diplomacy may lead to a continuation of the status quo. Eventually, social, economic, and political progress in the PRC may narrow the differences between the Mainland and Taiwan enough to make a "one China, two systems" alternative acceptable to all parties.

THE ENVIRONMENT

Modernization has taken a huge toll on the environment of China. According to the World Health Organization, seven of the ten most polluted cities in the world are in China, including the capital of Beijing. Labor complaints and pollution are the two leading causes of civil unrest.

According to the government's own figures, the air of two-thirds of China's 338 largest cities is either moderately or severely polluted. Diseases caused by air pollution represent the second leading cause of death in the PRC. China leads the world in the production of sulfur dioxide. An International Energy Agency report predicts that China will surpass the United States as the world's leading emitter of greenhouse gases by the end of 2007. The PRC signed the Kyoto Protocol on greenhouse gas emissions but, as a developing country, is largely exempt from the rules. So far, the government has refused to agree to limits on China's carbon dioxide emissions. However, the government is showing signs of increased action on emissions. In August 2007, Hu Jintao announced a massive reforestation plan to counterbalance carbon dioxide emissions while providing wood products lost in the destruction of so much forested land during The Great Leap Forward and the economic expansion of recent years.

Some 70% of China's energy production comes from the burning of coal. China is investing in cleaner alternatives, but coal will remain the mainstay of energy production for decades to come. Inefficient factories use far more energy than factories in the West to produce the same amount of such products as steel and cement. Unless China can import or develop technology that increases factory efficiency and allows the clean burning of its most plentiful energy resource, the cities will remain polluted and China will continue to pump huge amounts of greenhouse gases and other pollutants into the atmosphere. The pollution reaches far beyond China's borders. Carried by winds, China's particulate matter and acid rains fall on Korea, Japan, Taiwan, and even Los Angeles.

The glaciers that produce the Yangtze and many of China's other rivers are melting because of climate change. Some scientists predict that the glaciers may disappear in a century. A drought in the north has dried the Yellow River so that its waters no longer reach the sea in some years. In 2002, construction began on a massive pipeline system to divert water from the Yangtze to the water-starved north. The lines will follow three routes totaling some 2,300 miles (3,700 km), much of it over rugged terrain, to link China's four largest rivers, the Yangtze, Huang Ho (Yellow), Huaihe, and Haihe. As of 2007, 260 pollution control projects were underway to ensure the purity of the piped water. Completed in stages, the pipeline system will eventually carry 11.8 trillion gallons of water. Beijing will start receiving water in 2008 with final completion of the entire system scheduled for 2050, when it will be ten times the size of any of the world's current water diversion projects. Besides the estimated cost of $62 billion, there will be other prices to pay in the alteration of the Yangtze Valley environment and the relocation of an estimated 400,000 people.

**The mighty Huang Ho at Lanzhou, Gansu Province,
becomes a trickle by the time it reaches the sea.**

The effort to clean up the Yangtze is overdue. One 2006 study warned that without vigorous action, the great river would no longer support marine life by 2011. Already the huge Three Gorges dam project has drastically altered the river's environment. The hundreds of millions of people living in the Yangtze River Valley are increasingly affected by the river's pollution and the decline of once plentiful fish stocks.

According to the government, 70% of China's rivers are significantly polluted, making China's waters the dirtiest on the planet. Chinese industry uses 4 to 10 times more water than comparable factories in the West. Only about 50% of the sewage from China's cities is treated. The government is pushing to increase that figure to 70% by 2010. Current estimates are that the average Chinese has only about one quarter of the drinkable water per day that people enjoy in the industrialized West. In the north it is only about one eighth. An estimated 400 million Chinese lack regular access to clean water. One of China's greatest challenges is providing enough clean water in the decades ahead for human consumption and irrigation while keeping China's factories and vast waterborne transportation system viable.

The loss of cropland in a soil-poor country is another problem. Only about 10% of China's land is suitable for farming, but it is being squandered as cities sprawl outward. Highway, factory, and pipeline construction chews up more. Acid rain falls on 30% of the country, damaging cropland and water. Carcinogens in industrial waste have poisoned productive lands and created hundreds of "cancer villages."

In the spring and summer of 2007, China suffered an international loss of face when some of its consumer exports were declared unsafe. Inside the PRC, the problem is far worse. An estimated 300 million Chinese are sickened by food-borne illnesses yearly. A reported fifty babies died in 2004 from unsafe formula. With tens of thousands of new enterprises fighting for business, the government is scrambling to install efficient regulatory mechanisms to protect consumer safety. Until it succeeds, Chinese consumers and customers abroad will be at risk.

As always, population growth remains a huge worry. Already supporting four times the population of the United States on approximately the same amount of land—but without America's abundance of good farmland—China cannot sustain many more people. Government population experts hope to stabilize the population at about 1.6 billion people by 2050. Success will come none too soon.

After years of paying little attention to the environment, the government is moving vigorously to combat environmental degradation. But regulatory agencies are pitifully understaffed. Enforcement can be sidetracked by corruption or by provincial officials determined to pursue economic growth at any cost. Too often, regulations are simply ignored. An estimated 95% of China's new buildings do not meet government energy codes.

Still, there are some reasons to hope that the leadership of the PRC has accepted that China can no longer pursue economic expansion while ignoring the damage to the environment. In his 2007 address to the National People's Congress on the state of China, Premier Wen Jiabao made nearly fifty references to pollution and the environment on his way to sketching out ambitious new goals.

The PRC spends about 1% of its gross domestic product (GDP) on environmental issues, one of the leading rates in the world. The challenges remain immense but, with the commitment of the government and the willingness of the people to cooperate, the PRC may yet reverse the declining health of China's environment.

Shanghai

THE SOCIETY

Of all the changes wrought by modernization in China, probably the most profound is that people simply have more money. Deng Xiaoping's socialist market economy has lifted hundreds of millions from poverty and quadrupled family income. By various estimates 100 to 150 million people still live on less than a dollar a day, but the vast majority of the Chinese people have escaped the crushing poverty of the past. The availability of such basics as clothing, food, and shelter has markedly improved in a single generation. While few Chinese are rich, family incomes now permit such "luxuries" as stylish clothes, television sets, motor scooters, personal computers, cell phones, air conditioners, and refrigerators. Private car ownership, unknown thirty years ago, is booming. Ten people of every thousand own a car today—a tiny fraction compared to the American rate of 776 per 1,000—but ownership increased by 16% in the first six months of 2007 alone.

Modernization and the loosening of social controls have brought some undesirable changes. Crime, corruption, drug addiction, HIV/AIDS, and prostitution have all increased. Conservatives bewail the increase in divorce, premarital sex, and what they see as the decline of family and community traditions. Optimists tend to accept divorce and premarital sex as preferable to stultifying traditions where bad marriages were expected to endure and arranged marriages matched young people who barely knew each other.

The best of Confucian traditions seem as strong as ever. Increased prosperity and social mobility have challenged traditions, but the Chinese sense of family and community remains strong enough, in the view of optimists, to weather the changes brought by modernity. Like Japan, China will likely remain a deeply traditional society where family ties and community bonds provide the individual with identity and aid in good times and bad.

A confident government has loosened control over some civil rights, allowing freedom of speech and religion to a degree unknown in Mao's China. In 2004, the constitution was amended to guarantee the right to own and inherit private property. Fully 90% of villages have held elections, and the people's congresses at provincial and national levels are more assertive today. A survey in the late 1990's reported that 82% of Chinese were satisfied with their government. The increase in civil demonstrations indicates that this figure may have fallen. Yet the understanding that exists between the people and the Party—prosperity for power—seems to be holding.

If and for how the long the CCP can maintain its position remains very much open to question. Like any similar relationship known in past eras between peoples and authoritarian regimes, the control of the CCP may ultimately be vulnerable to the innate human drive to control one's own fate whatever the risks.

As the Olympic year dawns, some dark and threatening clouds hang on China's horizon. But, altogether, the forecast is bright, promising sunshine for the Chinese people in the 21st century.

Sources

GENERAL SOURCES

In writing *China: From the First Chinese to the Olympics*, I depended heavily on a number of general source works. Each of the following contributed something to nearly every chapter: Caroline Blunden and Mark Elvin, *Cultural Atlas of China* (New York: Facts on File, 1983); Alasdair Clayre, *The Heart of the Dragon* (Boston: Houghton Mifflin, 1985); Robert F. Dernberger et al., eds., *The Chinese: Adapting the Past, Building the Future* (Ann Arbor: University of Michigan Center for Chinese Studies, 1986); Keith Lye and Shirley Carpenter, eds., *Encyclopedia of World Geography* (New York: Dorset Press, 1989); John K. Fairbank, *China: A New History* (Cambridge, Mass.: Harvard University Pres, 1992); C. P. Fitzgerald, *China: A Short Cultural History*, 3rd ed. (New York: Holt, Rinehart & Winston, 1961), and *The Horizon History of China* (New York: American Heritage, 1969); John S. Major, *The Land and the People of China* (New York: J. B. Lippincott, 1989); National Geographic Society, *Journey into China* (Washington, D.C., 1982); Lucian W. Pye, *China: An Introduction* (Boston: Little, Brown, 1972); Jonathan D. Spence, *The Search for Modern China* (New York: W. W. Norton, 1990); Geoffrey Barraclough, ed., *The Times Concise Atlas of World History* (Maplewood, N. J.: Hammond, 1985).

ADDITIONAL SOURCES

Chapter 1, China: Most Populous Nation on Earth: *Beijing Review* (San Francisco: China Books); *China Briefing* (Boulder, Colo.: Westview Press, annual); *China Pictorial* (San Francisco: China Books); *China Today* (San Francisco: China Books); Beijing Municipal Commission of Urban Planning, <bjghw.gov.cn>; *Beijing Review*, <bjreview.cnmag.net>; Central Asia-Caucasus Institute, Silk Road Studies Program, <silkroadstudies.org>; China Business Review, <chinabusiness review.com>; China Development Gateway (Chinese Government and the Development Gateway Foundation), <en.chinagate.com>; China Knowledge, <chinaknowledge.com>; The Chinese Outpost <chinese-outpost.com> (particularly Chinapedia: <chinese-outpost.com/chinapedia>); *China Pictorial*, <rmhb.com.cn>; *China Today*, <chinatoday.com>; Chinability, <chinability.com>; Chinese Olympic Committee, <en.olympic.cn>; Encyclopaedia Britannica, <britannica.com>; Encyclopedia of the Nations, <nationsencyclopedia.com>; essortment, <nh.essortment.com>; Federation of American Scientists, <fas.org>; Futurecasts, <futurecasts.com>; Global Security Organization <globalsecurity.org>; Governments <gksoft.com/govt/en/cn.html> (lists websites of all government agencies); Information Please® Database, © 2007 Pearson Education, Inc., <infoplease.com>; *People's Daily*, <english.people.com.cn>; United Nations, <un.org>; United Nations Economic and Social Commission for Asia and the Pacific, <unescap.org>; Wikipedia, <en.wikipedia.org>; Women of China, <womenofchina.cn>; World Energy Organization, <worldenergy.org>.

Chapters 2 and 3, The First Chinese; Emperors, Dynasties, and Mandarins: Editors of Horizon Magazine, *The Horizon Book of the Arts of China* (New York: American Heritage, 1969); Walter A. Fairservis, Jr., *The Origins Of Oriental Civilization* (New York: New American Library, 1959); Edward H. Schafer, *Ancient China* (New York: Time-Life, 1967).

Chapter 4, Invaders from the North: Peter Brent, *Genghis Kahn: The Rise, Authority and Decline of Mongol Power* (New York: McGraw-Hill, 1976); Leo de Hartog, *Genghis Kahn: Conqueror of the World* (New York: St. Martin's, 1989).

Chapter 5, A Collision of Cultures: Burton F Beers, *China in Old Photographs, 1860–1910* (New York: Dorset Press, 1981); Maxine Hong Kingston, *The Woman Warrior* (New York: Alfred A. Knopf, 1977); *The Travels of Marco Polo* (New York: Orion, 1958); Alfred Tamarin and Shirley Glubok, *Voyaging to Cathay: Americans in the China Trade* (New York: Viking, 1976); Chester Tan, *The Boxer Catastrophe* (New York: Columbia University Press, 1955).

Chapter 6, Decades of Turmoil: Harrison E. Salisbury, *China: 100 Years of Revolution* (New York: Holt, Rinehart & Winston, 1983); Edgar Snow, *Red Star Over China,* rev. ed. (New York, Grove Press, 1989); Jonathan D. Spence, *The Gate of Heavenly Peace: The Chinese and Their Revolution, 1895-1980* (New York: Viking, 1981); Barbara W. Tuchman, *Stilwell and the American Experience in China, 1911-45* (New York: Macmillan, 1970); Dick Wilson, *When Tigers Fight: The Story of the Sino-Japanese War, 1937-1945* (New York: Viking, 1982).

Chapter 7, The Building of the People's Republic: Asia Research Centre, *The Great Cultural Revolution in China* (Rutland, Vt.: Charles E. Tuttle, 1968); Gordon A. Bennet and Ronald N. Montaperto, *Red Guard: The Political Biography of Dai Hsiao-Ai* (New York: Doubleday, 1971); David Wen-Wei Chang, *Zhou Enlai and Deng Xiaoping in the Chinese Leadership Succession Crisis* (Lanham, Md.: University Press of America, 1984); Han Suyin, *Wind in the Tower: Mao Tsetung and the Chinese Revolution, 1949-1975* (Boston: Little, Brown, 1976); W. J. F. Jenner, ed., *China: A Photohistory 1937–1987* (New York: Pantheon, 1988); Liang Heng and Judith Shapiro, *Son of the Revolution* (New York: Alfred A. Knopf, 1983); *Quotations from Chairman Mao Tse-Tung* (New York: Bantam, 1967).

Chapter 8, The Pragmatists Triumph: David Wen-Wei Chang, *China Under Deng Xiaoping: Political and Economic Reform* (New York: St. Martin's, 1988); Uli Franz, *Deng Xiaoping* (Orlando, Fla.: Harcourt Brace Jovanovich, 1988); John Frazer, *The Chinese: Portrait of a People* (New York, Summit Books, 1980); Ross Terrill, ed., *The China Difference* (New York: Harper & Row, 1979).

Chapters 9, The Democracy Movement: Associated Press, *China from the Long March to Tiananmen Square* (New York: Henry Holt, 1990); Fang Lizhi, *Bringing Down the Great Wall: Writings on Science, Culture and Democracy in China* (New York: Alfred A. Knopf, 1991); Human Rights in China, *Children of the Dragon* (New York: Collier Books, 1990); Liu Binyan, *Tell the World: What Happened in China and Why* (New York: Pantheon, 1989), and *China's Crisis, China's Hope: Essays from an Intellectual in Exile* (Cambridge, Mass.: Harvard University Press, 1990);

Andrew J. Nathan, *China's Crisis: Dilemmas of Reform and Prospects for Democracy* (New York: Columbia University Press, 1990); Scott Simmie and Bob Nixon, *Tiananmen Square* (Seattle: University of Washington Press, 1989).

Chapter 10, Hard-liners and Pragmatists: Joseph Fewsmith, *China Since Tiananmen: The Politics of Transition* (New York: Cambridge University Press, 2001); John Gittings, *The Changing Face of China: From Mao to Market* (New York: Oxford University Press, 2005).

Chapters 11 and 12: China and the World; China's Century? see sources for Chapters 1 and 10.

Suggested Reading

NONFICTION

Associated Press. *China from the Long March to Tiananmen Square.*
New York: Henry Holt, 1990.

Beers, Burton F. *China in Old Photographs, 1860–1910.* New York:
Dorset Press, 1981.

Blunden, Caroline, and Mark Elvin. *Cultural Atlas of China.* New
York: Facts on File, 1983.

China Briefing. Boulder, Colo.: Westview Press, annual.

China: The Land and the People. New York: Gallery Books, 1988.

Clayre, Alasdair. *The Heart of the Dragon.* Boston: Houghton Mifflin,
1985.

Editors of Horizon Magazine. *The Horizon Book of the Arts of China.*
New York: American Heritage, 1969.

Fitzgerald, C. P. *The Horizon History of China.* New York: American
Heritage, 1969.

Human Rights in China. *Children of the Dragon.* New York: Collier
Books, 1990.

Jenner, W. J. F., ed. *China: A Photohistory 1937–1987.* New York:
Pantheon, 1988.

Kingston, Maxine Hong. *The Woman Warrior.* New York: Alfred A.
Knopf, 1977.

Major, John S. *The Land and the People of China.* New York: J. B. Lippincott, 1989.

National Geographic Society. *Journey into China.* Washington, D.C., 1982.

Pye, Lucian W. *China: An Introduction.* Boston: Little, Brown, 1972.

Salisbury, Harrison E. *China: 100 Years of Revolution.* New York: Holt, Rinehart & Winston, 1983.

Schafer, Edward H. *Ancient China.* New York: Time-Life, 1967.

Sinclair, Kevin. *Over China.* Los Angeles: Knapp Press, 1988.

FICTION

Birch, Cyril, ed. *Anthology of Chinese Literature.* New York: Evergreen Books, 1965.

Buck, Pearl S. *The Good Earth.* New York: John Day, 1931.

Hersey, John. *A Single Pebble.* New York: Alfred A. Knopf, 1956.

Lao She. *Cat Country.* William A. Lyell, Jr., trans. Columbus: Ohio State University Press, 1970.
_____. *Rickshaw.* Jean M. James, trans. Honolulu: University Press of Hawaii, 1979.

Lord, Bette Bao. *Spring Moon.* New York: Harper & Row, 1981.

Tan, Amy. *The Joy-Luck Club.* New York: Putnam, 1989.

TELEVISION AND FILM

Good Earth, The. Sidney Franklin, director. United States: 1937.

Great Wall, A. Peter Wang, director. United States and China: 1986.

Heart of the Dragon, The. Public Broadcasting System. United States: 1985.

Ju Dou. Ahang Yi-mou, director. China and Japan: 1989.

Last Emperor, The. Bernard Bertolucci, director. United States, Great Britain, Italy, and China: 1987.

Morning Sun. Carma Hinton, Geremie Barmé, and Richard Gordon, directors. United States and China, 2003.

Sand Pebbles, The. Robert Wise, director. United States: 1966.

Printed in the United States
115203LV00001B/180/P